The *Starfish* from *Africa*

The Story of Yannick Kabuguza and
The Power of Forgiveness

By William J. Lavin

Where Angels Play Foundation
PO Box 670
Oakhurst, NJ 07755
whereangelsplayfoundation.org

ISBN: 978-1-7923-5478-6

Front cover design by Yannick Kabuguza

Prooceeds of this book will go directly to the Where Angels Play Foundation to continue our mission bringing joy to communities around the world. For more information on how to contribute, go to whereangelsplayfoundation.org.

Dedication

This Book is dedicated to the Power of forgiveness,
the amazing view afforded those who find the strength to stand in the
shoes of an adversary, and the understanding that immediately follows.

For Teddy, Juni, Matty and Will and children all over the world.

Table of Contents

Starfish on the Beach

Based on the writings of Loren Eiseley

An old man had a habit of early morning walks on the beach. One day, after a storm, he saw a human figure in the distance moving like a dancer. As he came closer he saw that it was a young woman and she was not dancing but was reaching down to the sand, picking up starfish and very gently throwing them into the ocean. "Young lady," he asked, "why are you throwing starfish into the ocean?"

She replied, "the sun is up, and the tide is going out and if I do not throw them in they will die."

"Do you not realize that there are miles and miles of beach and starfish all along it? You cannot possibly make a difference," he responded.

The young woman listened politely, paused, and then bent down, picked up another starfish and threw it into the sea, past the breaking waves, saying,

"It made a difference for that one."

From the Author

Hello reader,

Welcome to the *Starfish from Africa* and thank you for opening this book and being curious enough to start to read this story. The fact that you have this book in your hands is my blessing and my challenge that by the time you finish this story it will feel like your blessing as well.

As a much more experienced reader than writer, I fully recognize that this moment is my opportunity to "set the hook," and gain your interest enough to have you read on to the next chapter so that this remarkable story becomes a part of your life and a part of your story-telling. I hope to make you interested enough in this story that you will continue to turn the pages and learn not only about a young man's survival but how I have come to know about it and why it's important enough for you to know about it as well.

This story is all true despite the fact that there will be times when you and I will wish it were not true and that it never happened. But hopefully there will also be times that you will be glad and quite inspired that this story is true and actually took place exactly as it is written.

As you read on, please remember that this is real life, real tragedy, real meanness, real cruelty, real suffering, and real sadness. If you accept all of the above you will come to understand what is also real... triumph, joy, compassion, generosity, healing, survival and perhaps the greatest gift to ones self, forgiveness. Triumph and redemption are possible and far more powerful than any challenge or difficulty.

If I can do half the job this story deserves, you will be changed forever, not because I am an amazing writer but rather, despite my limitations, this story tells itself.

This is a story that needs to be told and needs to be told now more than ever.

Hopefully this story will capture, not only your attention, but your heart and inspire you the way it has inspired me as well as all the other characters of whom you are about to meet. I ask for your indulgence, your patience and your time. In return I promise you honesty, and inspiration and a story I believe you will be compelled to want to share with others.

As you begin this journey with me and young Yannick Kabuguza, I ask that you open your heart and your mind to experience the story with the very real understanding, it is sadly and happily true, and has the potential to change us all for the better.

My sincere thanks for your trust and time. I am anxious for you to get to know my *Starfish from Africa*.

The Land of a Thousand Hills

Rwanda is one of the smallest countries in Africa. Located near the eastern central portion of the continent, Rwanda is one of the most densely populated.

Roughly the size of Vermont in size, Rwanda has 20 times the population. In comparison, Rwanda's population is over 12 million as opposed to Vermont having just over 600,000 residents.

Known for its beautiful landscape of green mountains and valleys, Rwanda is sometimes referred to as the "Switzerland of Africa". Kibeho, Rwanda the site of the visitation of the Virgin Mary is over 6,000 feet above sea level.

Lush green mountains and valleys make Rwanda a breathtakingly beautiful country. With the exception of the capital city of Kigali, Rwanda is predominantly rural and impoverished. Subsistence farming is the main economic form of survival for Rwandans. Outside of Kigali the roadways are very primitive. Mostly dirt roads lead into and surround the village of Kibeho.

Bus travel, mopeds and taxis are the main mode of transportation. Many Rwandans who live in the southern provinces of Rwanda will rarely, if ever, leave their villages.

The beautiful country of Rwanda and its amazing wildlife of mountain gorillas and golden monkeys provide breathtaking scenery and conjure up peaceful and wondrous thoughts. It is impossible, however, to not feel the undercurrent of Rwanda's past fraught with grief, loss and sadness.

The people of Rwanda greet you with an initial wariness and some trepidation. Some have said, the people of Rwanda "cry their tears from the inside." But a smile or a friendly greeting directed at a Rwandan citizen is often met with a burst of joy and great happiness.

It becomes quite evident to many visitors that the Rwandan people are longing for friendship, love and understanding. The story of the Starfish from Africa underscores the resilience of the Rwandan people and their great desire to heal, recover and prosper.

Historical Background

While this story is not meant to provide a history lesson or a political perspective of the country of Rwanda, it is necessary to provide some context for the reader regarding the names of the clans involved and the unrest that supported the environment necessary to allow for genocide and unspeakable atrocities.

Since at least the 1950's, Rwanda experienced civil unrest between its inhabitants. There were three main ethnic classifications in Rwanda. The majority of Rwandans, approximately 80%, were referred to as Hutu. The Hutu were described as stocky of build with wide noses and usually of darker pigmentation. Tutsi, who comprise about 15% of the population were thought to be lighter skinned, had sharper noses and facial features, and were usually taller and more slender of build. The Twa clan, are a group of pygmies that are considerably shorter than other Rwandans and largely stay among themselves and comprise the balance of the population

It should be noted, the idea that you can tell a Hutu or a Tutsi by their physical appearance is largely a myth propagated by the Germans and Belgians. The selective process of recruitment of individuals into administrative posts of the occupying governments accounts for such stereotyping. If you were tall and more European looking, they labeled you Tutsi. If you were darker and had broader noses you were labeled

Hutu. And of course the Twa Pygmy people were quite short and dark and were considered the surviving ancestral tribe of the East African Great Lakes region.

The labeling and distinctions associated with physical traits falsely translating to intelligence and or economic status created racist myths that served to alienate Rwandans from one another.

Animosity between the Tutsi and Hutu existed for many reasons. Suffice it to say when the Tutsi clan was in power resentment grew among the majority Hutu faction. Rumors of planned extermination and oppression continued for years among the Rwandan people. Ironically, marriage and interaction between Hutus and Tutsi's was very common. When the Tutsi's eventually controlled much of the wealth in Rwanda, natural jealousies began and as poverty worsened among the Hutus, hatred festered among the people.

In April 1994, when President Juvenal Habyarimana's plane was shot down, it triggered Hutu extremists to begin the Genocide of all Tutsi citizens whom they blamed for the president's death. The responsibility for shooting down President Habyarimana's plane is still the subject of controversy and is still very much debated to this day. This incident sparked the killing of almost one million Rwandan's, mostly Tutsi and Hutu sympathizers. Gruesome and mindless, this genocide provides the backdrop for a remarkable story of survival, forgiveness and perseverance.

While the story of Yannick Kabuguza is incredible, it serves as only one example of the countless stories of survival and "triumph over tragedy" of so many of the Rwandan people.

This story is dedicated to the spirit of the Rwandan people and all those who suffered and died in the horrific genocide there and in genocides around the world. May Yannick Kabuguza and the story of the "Starfish from Africa" provide hope and inspiration for all oppressed and downtrodden people around the world.

PART I

Tragedy

Written by Bill Lavin as told to by Yannick Kabuguza

"Hate is like a poison you drink expecting the other person to die."

— *Nelson Mandela*

CHAPTER ONE

Madness

He sat in the middle of his living room area on a dirt floor playing with the bugs that trafficked between his legs. He could hear his mother's beautiful singing voice telling tales of joyful days spent in the beautiful Rwandan countryside. Yannick, and his cousin, Penti, played happily together. Penti and Yannick were almost exactly the same age and they got along with one another very well. Penti loved to pretend he was a soldier and taught Yannick to mimic the soldiers they would see around their neighborhood. Yannick and Penti would march around the house pretending to shoot one another, diving over furniture and practicing their dramatic fake deaths. *War games were fun,* Yannick thought, and Penti could not be a better partner to play out their imaginative battles. When the game ended, Yannick and Penti would always be victorious over their imaginary enemies.

The smell of rice and vegetables steaming was filling the air. It was Sunday, and the Kabuguza family was preparing a typical Sunday Rwandan dinner. Times were not great with the Rwandan economy in early April 1994, although Yannick's family always seemed to make the best of it.

Grandma and Grandpa would cook the best foods in the country. For all Yannick knew, he was a normal, happy little boy with toys and an imagination to keep him content and satisfied as much as possible while living in the beautiful East African country of Rwanda.

At three and a half years old, Yannick was just starting to appreciate how beautiful his Mom was. She was so full of joy and energy and seemed to never stop smiling. Claudine was so young and hadn't realized what her life might be like without the responsibility of caring for a small child. Thankfully, Grandma and Grandpa were quite respected in the community and had provided a roof over the head of their daughter, Claudine, and their grandson Yannick. Yannick's dad, who he rarely saw or remembered, lived with his wife and four other children in a village some distance away. Yannick would learn later on in his life that Claudine's situation was not unusual for the area. Rwandan men often had multiple wives and many children. Relationships, Yannick would also learn, for Rwandans were much more a function of survival and economics.

If a man could afford to support a woman and a child, subsequent relationships were not frowned upon by anyone in Rwandan society. Looks, attraction, and affection, often were sacrificed for survival and practicality. If the economics were favorable to a man it mattered little what he looked like, but rather, whether or not he could provide for a young woman and remove her from poverty and provide a modicum of independence from her parents. Yannicks' Mom and Dad's relationship was somewhat the norm.

Yannick's Grandfather was retired from the National Park Ranger Service and he was home a lot. The memories Yannick had of him were of a strong, serious and very kind man. Bosco, as Grandpa was called, had earned the respect of his neighbors. He was a law-abiding citizen; a proud Rwandan man who prided himself on being able to provide for himself and his family. Yannick's family was slightly better off financially and the neighbors would often ask to borrow tools and supplies from Bosco who was known as a generous man and always willing to share whatever extra items he had.

Yannick and Penti began to play with their one prized possession. It was a ball of plastic made up of some old bottles, some pieces of plastic wrapping and some caps from containers that once held food, all thrown together with skill by his Grandpa Bosco. They were crushed together into a crinkly ball of silver and green colored wonder. Kicking the ball, balancing it on their heads, throwing it against the wall and playing catch with Bosco or Yannick's Mom were some of the boys' earliest happy memories. That wonderful collection of trash recycled into a tight ball could rival any mass-produced professionally made sports equipment. Running around outside with it, kicking it from his foot to his knee, bouncing it and eventually falling asleep with it under his arm made him feel such joy. When Yannick was with his soccer ball, he didn't have a care in the world. Yannick rested on some soft blankets that had been tossed in the corner of the room and drifted off to sleep.

CRASH!!!

Suddenly, the room exploded with noise and Yannick was startled out of his sleep. Yelling and screaming reverberated everywhere. The front door crashed open followed by a rush of crazed men, eyes red and bulging, screaming at the top of their lungs. These men were swinging dirty, rusty machetes. Yannick was thrown into the corner of the room and he was covered partly by chairs and an overturned table. The room continued to fill with men, wearing half soldier uniforms and half civilian clothes. Some men had either military pants or shirts, but not both.

The screams of his grandparents continued over the shouts of the fake soldiers. Blood began to spray everywhere, splattering the walls and furniture. Sick and painful cries echoed, over and over throughout the room. Yannick watched in horror from his unplanned, unintentional hiding place. With what must have been the explosion of grenades, or some military explosives going off in and around the house, the ringing in Yannick's ears was overwhelming and deafening.

Screams grew eerily silent, replaced by twisted facial expressions showing tortured looks of fear and terror. The smell of smoke, dust, dirt and gunpowder filled his nostrils. The horrified expressions of surprise, featured eyes bulging with fear then horror. Then the blood seemed to splatter everywhere, almost as, in slow motion.

Skin, bone and body parts filled the air and littered the floor. Out of the corner of his eye, Yannick saw Penti running out the back door.

The stunned faces of Bosco and Grandma were staring at Yannick, and his mom. Yannick's attention now focused on his mom Claudine.

Yannick watched his mother forcibly held down by the strange men, intent on hurting her. Frozen, as if in shock, Yannick could only stare in confusion.

Yannick realized that Claudine was being stripped of her clothes and brutally violated. Claudine bravely struggled to fight off her attackers, but there were too many strong men with crazed looks in their eyes filled with hate and contempt. The more she struggled, the more they beat her. The more she screamed, the more they laughed. Yannick thought how ugly and distorted the faces of these men were. Then suddenly, one wild, small, animal of a man, pulled a large knife from his belt plunging its blade deep into Claudine's belly.

The force was so great it went right through her and Claudine fell over as if broken in half. The crazy-eyed animal repeatedly stabbed her over and over again, until her body lay lifeless. Yannick stared frozen in place, unable to move or cry or turn away. He just stared at what was left of his mom, completely confused as to what in the world was happening.

Just then, a familiar face appeared before Yannick. The neighbor, Kayibanda who lived next door and often ate meals at the house and drank beer with Yannick's grandfather stood before him. But something was different about him now. His eyes were bulging out of his head and were all red and scary. He seemed to be crying as well. His mouth was distorted as if he threatened to bite Yannick. At first, Yannick thought Kayibanda was reaching down to pick him up as he had often done many times in the past. Instead, a flash of metal blinded Yannick for an instant. Then Yannick saw a streak of light and heard a strange clacking sound as he fell to the floor.

Yannick lay on the floor and everything went dark, as if the lights and the sun had been blocked out of the sky. He pushed himself back up to his knees, and felt wet on his chest and his pants. He wondered if he had urinated all over himself.

Suddenly a searing burn seemed to split his face in two. Yannick felt heat, then a dull ache, and now a shuttering, shaking, stabbing pain driving through his face and he thought his head was splitting into two pieces. Yannick reached up to the left side of his face and felt there was a hole in his head. He pulled his hand down to look at it and found something soft like a small ball in his hand that was now red with blood.

He suddenly realized, he was looking at a large piece of his left ear. The pain was beginning to grow. The air seemed to be blowing through his brain. He tried to put his hand with the piece of ear back onto his head. He then looked back up at his attacker Kayibanda who seemed to be in as much shock as Yannick.

Kayibanda raised the machete over his head once again and froze. He stared wildly at Yannick as if horrified by the sight and result of his first blow. He slammed down his arm and weapon with incredible force and cut the top of the kitchen table in half. He cried out and wept like a man in great agony. Maybe he realized the horror of his own action. Maybe God had steered his hand away from cutting off the head of this small boy who stood in front of him. But something profound happened at that moment. Kayibanda picked up Yannick and carried him through the chaos of smoke and fire. Kayibandi stepped over Claudine's body and what looked like a hand or foot. Then the room went black.

Yannick's Mother and family memorialized after the genocide

CHAPTER TWO

An Angel of Mercy

Like a thick cloud evaporating, the room slowly grew lighter. The room was different than before. Yannick remembered this place was the living room of his neighbor across the street. The pain in Yannick's head pounded like the drum he remembered from the radio station his Grandpa Bosco once listened. Only this pounding was in the center of his brain. Thick liquid dripped continuously into Yannick's mouth. He tried to swallow it but it was thick and clumpy. He choked and spit out the mess that was filling his throat. Through his right eye he managed to see that it was bright red with brown clumps. He realized his own blood was trying to choke him.

The makeshift bandage that was now wrapped around his head and most of his face oozed with fresh blood mixing with dried cartilage and pieces of bone to form a heavy, wet helmet on Yannick's face and skull. He cried out but no sound was made. The pain was relentless. Boom. Boom. Boom. Boom. Louder and louder, boom, boom, boom boom! It echoed until he attempted another scream that also fell silent and drove Yannick to pass out once again.

Waking to shouts of panic Yannick heard his name called over and over. He tried to pick his head up but the pain, like a knife, drove deep into his head as if his skull would break in two. Karigo, Yannick's beautiful twenty-year old neighbor, who sometimes looked after him, could hear the shouts of soldiers at the door. She was attempting to pick Yannick up and place his skinny, bloody body over her shoulder. Yannick vomited blood onto her back, but she had no time to notice. Carrying Yannick through the house to the backyard, she hid him in the thick brush. Yannick vomited again and moaned in excruciating pain. Karigo ran back into the house as Yannick watched and tried to call after her but again no sound was made. Karigo met the Hutu soldiers in the front of Yannick's house shouting to them to stop banging on the front door and shutters.

As Karigo opened the door they pushed passed her and ran through the house as if searching for a loose animal.

"Where is that little cockroach?" one shouted.

"We know he is in here," said another.

"We heard that you carried him here, where is he?"

They shouted and searched and searched while Karigo assured them he wasn't there. She pretended to sympathize with them, telling them that, being Hutu, she too hated the Tutsis and fully supported the killing of any and all who threatened the future of her Hutu people.

She offered them food and drink and they greedily accepted her offer which seemed to calm them down until they finally left the house, saying, "You must report any Tutsi cockroach that you see, especially the little ones for they will exact vengeance against us in the future if we allow even one of them to survive."

She feigned disgust at the thought of even one Tutsi surviving. They then left as quickly as they had arrived.

By the time Karigo returned to the backyard, Yannick was missing. He was no longer lying in the thicket where she had left him. "Oh God!" She worried that the soldiers had found him and taken him away. Then she heard a faint rustling in the reeds. Yannick's legs were sticking out of the green grass and a neighbors' dog was biting his legs and licking the blood from his body. Karigo shooed the dog away as quickly as she could, picked up Yannick and returned him to the bed inside her home.

Days passed and Karigo had changed Yannick's bandage countless times. To call these rags dressings is quite a stretch but slowly Karigo noticed the oozing of blood slowing down. After a week, it was down to a trickle. Yannick drank some water Karigo had forced down his throat but he hadn't eaten a thing for over a week. He was groggy and unsteady and struggled to sit up.

Soon Karigo was able to get Yannick to stand and take some steps. This, however, caused his gaping wound to gush blood through his bandage. She immediately laid him back down. Karigo attempted several times a day to have Yannick stand and walk, until finally one day he took some steps without falling or passing out. When Karigo was able to get Yannick to eat some pieces of bread, she thought that maybe, just maybe, he might live another week.

'This routine continued until Yannick was strong enough to walk on his own. He still had not uttered a word since the attack. Knowing she had to get Yannick out of her house and to safety before the soldiers returned she forced him to eat and drink and religiously changed his bandages. Karigo herself would often get sick to her stomach from the sight and smell of this gaping wound that cut deep through his left ear and his cheek. Karigo could see right through to the other side of his mouth. The fact that Yannick was still alive was no small miracle. Karigo began to believe that he might have been spared by God to live for another purpose. What that purpose was she could never imagine.

Three weeks passed and Karigo remarkably not only kept Yannick hidden but had nourished him just enough so that he could now walk and go to the bathroom on his own.

She knew it was time to make a move, not only for Yannick's sake, but also for herself. Karigo was a Hutu, and she needed to leave the area as soon as possible as the Tutsi rebel forces were closing in on the area. It would not be safe for her or anyone really. Kigali held no place for her anymore. The killings, grenades, shooting, blood, smell of death and hate and sadness were everywhere. Karigo felt trapped in Kigali and disgusted by her neighbors, never believing that her fellow man, fellow Africans, fellow Hutus, could ever be so heartless, so savage and so cruel. Karigo, knew she had to find another place to live... where exactly, she really didn't care!

One morning, Karigo grabbed whatever clothes, food and supplies she could strap onto her back and carry on her head. She grabbed Yannick by the hand and headed out to the main roadway. It was dawn and most of the neighborhood was quiet. She knew there was a bus that eventually led to the border of Burundi and felt that that was her best opportunity for a new life and a chance for survival for her and her new responsibility, young Yannick. *How could she keep him alive when she could barely fend for herself?* she thought.

As silently as they could they made their way out of the front yard and began walking, limping and stumbling toward the main bus stop. Karigo was glad that no one else was up so early and the bus stop was empty and eerily void of life. At least an hour went by and the humidity began to grow and the air became thick and steamy. Yannick could barely keep his eyes open. Karigo prayed that the bus would arrive soon, and a new life could begin for her and her young companion.

The rumble in the distance and clatter of metal on stones signaled the approach of the rickety old commuter bus. As the bus neared, Karigo could see that it was full of people with bobbing heads and eyeballs all trained on her and young Yannick. The bus came to a gradual stop as if every person on the bus needed to inspect the new potential passengers. As the door opened and the driver peered over passengers at Karigo and Yannick, he put the vehicle in park and jumped to his feet.

Meanwhile, the passengers began to yell for him to continue without stopping as they were already beyond capacity and had no room for any more passengers. The driver seemed to take pity on Yannick and Karigo and began to help both of them into the front of the bus where there was a tiny bit of space to squeeze another passenger.

Just then a woman yelled at Yannick, "He is an injured cockroach and will bleed on us all."

Another yelled, "He will bring death to us."

"He is Tutsi scum and will have us all be murdered by the soldiers!" an old man shouted.

"Move out. Do not let that cockroach on this bus or we shall all surely be cut to pieces by the soldiers at the roadblock."

Yannick stared in silence and could barely hear or understand what they were saying but he could see clearly that their angry faces meant him harm and cared little for him or Karigo.

Finally, the driver said to Karigo, "I can see you are Hutu like us and we have room for you, but this boy has been wounded gravely and is obviously a Tutsi."

He continued, "I cannot risk the lives of all my passengers and they will surely not allow him to get on this bus. You must make a decision to come by yourself and leave this boy behind or you will not be allowed to travel with us. It is just too dangerous," he warned.

Karigo's heart sank as she looked at the pathetic sight of this young boy with the red bandages oozing blood and he could barely stand. She pressed his head against her leg, cried bitterly and said a prayer for God to forgive her and then she jumped onto the bus that was already in motion. Yannick fell backward and could only stare through the dust of the road as the bus pulled away with the crowd of Rwandans who were now silent as they watched this little boy disappear around the bend of the road.

"He will surely die of his wounds soon anyway," one woman said.

"Do not feel for him. Only God can help him now," said a voice trailing off against the roar of the motor.

Yannick watched the bus pull away as Karigo cried loudly. Yannick felt his life and any chance of survival rolling slowly away from him.

Men of Kibeho gather for a meeting

CHAPTER THREE

I Have Seen Him in the Watch Fires of a Hundred Circling Camps

Too tired and in too much pain to feel any emotion, Yannick stumbled into a field of tall grass. It was soft enough to lie down in, and was certainly cooler than the sunny opening at the bus stop. He slept for how long he did not know. When he awoke, he heard the sound of laughter and the yelling of men's voices arguing and shouting. The men seemed to all talk at the same time. Yannick knew these men were dressed the same as those who had attacked him, his mother, and grand parents so he crawled further into the grass so as to be out of sight. He listened to the men as they marched by haphazardly. They seemed evil to him, full of hate. For all he knew, they represented danger to Yannick. He knew he must stay far away from them or they would hurt him even more than he had been hurt already.

Swatting mosquitoes and bugs he didn't recognize, Yannick peered from the grass as if he were a lion or large cat waiting for some prey to come by. The pain in his head was constant now but somehow he managed to keep his eyes open. He realized that his hearing was slowly coming back to him. But a constant ringing and buzzing dominated his thoughts.

Night fell and growls and sounds of the bush kept him awake until he could no longer keep his eyes open. He fell into a deep slumber and dreamt his mom was bathing him in a beautiful clear lake and his grandparents were making a delicious dinner off to the side.

Finally, Yannick woke to the sound of a nearby rooster crowing its morning cock-a-doodle-doo. He immediately realized that his mom and grandparents were no longer alive and he was truly alone in the world. For the first time since the attack he began to cry, first softly, then he wept and shook and shuttered uncontrollably. Tears flowed like a faucet until his shirt and pants were completely soaked. He was wet from front to back and thought he might have wet himself but cared little and continued to weep.

Suddenly a white Jeep roared past, followed by what Yannick thought were more Hutu soldiers. He crawled through the grass but this time he could not avoid being seen by the men in uniform. They had a large red cross on their white shirts and spoke a very different language. These men were white. *How strange,* Yannick thought. They looked and spoke and carried themselves very differently. One man who had seen Yannick approached him and smiled. *What a strange sight,* Yannick thought to himself but somehow he felt that these men were not here to hurt him. They surrounded Yannick and they all seemed to marvel at him and spoke rapidly to one another. After a few minutes, Yannick was convinced that these men would help him. He hugged them and felt sad and ashamed that he had gotten his blood on the uniform of his rescuers.

These men, as it turned out, were from the Red Cross. They carried Yannick onto their Jeep and drove him to a refugee camp that was guarded by men with large guns. The camp was much cleaner than any of the war torn houses Yannick had seen along the walk to the bus and along the ride he had taken in the Jeep.

His country of Rwanda was a mess—a pile of rubble of houses burned out with bullet-ridden walls. Bodies littered the roadway in the front yards of neighborhood houses. Wild dogs, just trying to survive, were eating the rotting corpses of men women and children. This horrific sight was only surpassed by the ever-sickening smell and sounds of death. A country of love and beauty and song and wonderful nature was now a rotting collage of hate, death, grief and sadness. All Yannick could think of was that he needed desperately to get as far away from his former home as possible.

The camp seemed to have some order to it. Tents, makeshift beds, and cooking stations were all filled with people. Many were wounded and dying. Many others, however, were unhurt, at least physically, and were taking care of the injured. Finally, Yannick thought, people are showing some compassion and kindness to one another.

Except for the constant pain of his wounds and the medical personnel constantly pulling, cleaning and prodding at his head and face, Yannick began to think that maybe somehow he wouldn't be left to die. Although many times Yannick wished he were dead along with his mom and grandparents. He knew they were in a better place. He continued to slowly get stronger and began to eat food and drink water on a more regular basis. Camp life was not perfect by any means. While Yannick witnessed acts of kindness toward other people by the Red Cross workers and United Nations soldiers, most Rwandan people turned their heads away from him, either in disgust or perhaps unwilling to be reminded of the cruelty that their fellow countrymen were capable of doing. If such brutality could be exacted upon a small child, what other unspeakable atrocities could be possible?

This feeling that Yannick had was a painful reminder and a grotesque example of the horrors of the Rwandan genocide. It would stick with him for his entire childhood and early adulthood. He knew by looking in the eyes of others that they saw in him a walking, talking, living reminder of a hideous legacy of the Rwandan people.

For the next year and a half Yannick woke up in pain and discomfort watching the world play out in refugee camps in Rwanda and neighboring Burundi. He saw life from the very edge of survival mode. He hoped to have enough to eat, drink and clothe himself, even if it were only rags on his body to keep him somewhat covered. He fought infection as the wound caused by the machete never medically healed... he had no stiches, staples or anything remotely resembling medical care.

The wound became a scab, that became a scar, that became an open wound again, then a scab, then an infection and so on and so on.

His pain ebbed and flowed and revisited him like a miserable old evil fiend over and over again. He suffered constantly with headaches, vision problems, hearing issues, not to mention the constant discrimination. His own tribe avoided him and continually shunned him and turned their eyes away from him.

Yannick occasionally was treated with compassion but he rarely experienced friendship from other children. He often spent time kicking and heading a homemade soccer ball whenever the camp made that available to him. Surviving was his past time. Winning each day to just arrive at the next morning was his ritual. Social interaction was limited but Yannick listened to every word that was spoken. Whether it was in his mother's tongue of Kinyarwanda, French, Swahili, or the English language of the Red Cross workers. He listened, rarely spoke, but he listened and learned the languages that surrounded him.

He was a young boy with a scar on his face and head, but a mind that was sharp, keen, hungry, and beautiful—a mind that absorbed everything he heard, saw, and felt. Yannick was a young boy who learned to navigate the refugee camp society. He learned how to be invisible, while seeing more than anyone else.

Children of Rwanda greet visitors from the roadside

A sign from heaven marks the location of the new playground

A sea of humanity gathers to honor "Our Lady of Kibeho"

CHAPTER FOUR

I Was Lost, Now I'm Found

For almost two years, Yannick was shifted from one refugee camp to another. Through Burundi and Rwanda, Yannick survived by staying out of the way of other people. He ate when it was possible and had his facial wound cared for from time to time. Infection of his facial wounds was a constant and recurring problem. Gangrene set in several times and, thankfully, he was given antibiotics to kill the infection. These medicines always made Yannick sick to his stomach. Severe stomach cramps, diarrhea, and vomiting were a common occurrence for Yannick. He remained dangerously thin and his growth and physical improvement was slow to come. He often felt weak and only occasionally did he feel well or strong enough to play soccer, the game he was learning to love very much.

Yannick continued to survive day after very long day. From time to time he would get to communicate and play with other children refugees who were mostly from Rwanda and Tutsi like himself. But Yannick also met many others from surrounding countries who spoke Swahili, French, English and, of course, Kinyarwanda, his native tongue. He got his education through his language skills. He began to understand and learn so many things just by listening and being an observer from the many secret-hiding places he would find and/or create. Yannick amused himself by trying to be almost invisible and watching others. He studied how people communicated with each other. He learned how to find extra food or supplies all by understanding the personal nuances between the cultures, and because he understood more languages than most of the other children his age. He kept many secrets to himself that amused him and that he used to his advantage to ultimately keep himself alive.

In spring 1996, the government of Rwanda began to gather information about the many people who were still living in the refugee camps in and around the Rwandan border. After the names were gathered, along with the appropriate ages and descriptions of the inhabitants of these camps, the national radio network would announce the refugees' information over the radio airwaves across the countryside but mainly in the capital city of Kigali. The name of five-year-old Yannick Kabuguza was included.

Unbeknownst to Yannick, at their small Kigali home his aunt Goretti and her husband Peter were caring for their newborn son Beradi. Goretti often listened to the radio to get any news regarding the new political regime of Rwandan President Kagame. Being the sister of Claudine, Yannick's mom and having lost her parents to the genocide as well, Goretti was keenly aware of the current political climate. After the genocide had ended, General Paul Kagame came to power, after leading the resistance and crushing the Hutu army extremists who had visited so much evil and death upon the citizens of Rwanda. Goretti paid close attention to the news around the country.

Over the course of the previous 18 months, the rest of the world was grappling with what had happened in Rwanda. Countries, like the United States of America, questioned how such a catastrophe could take place in this day and age, without any intervention. The international community was appalled and blame and finger pointing filled the news. The Rwandan Genocide revealed itself to be, one of the worst examples in world history of man's inhumanity to man. Rwandan National Radio provided Goretti and Peter constant news of the slow economic and social recovery of Rwanda. Peter and Goretti wanted to be a part of the recovery and take every advantage they could, to assist them as they started their new family.

The prosecution of war criminals, as well as the new Rwandan policy that eliminated the classification of Hutu and Tutsi from all personal identification, was an exciting initiative of the new government.

President Kagame signed an executive order to declare every citizen Rwandan, and they would forever only be Rwandan, not Tutsi or Hutu ever again. A message of, "One Rwanda for All," was adopted.

As the radio turned its report from politics to the refugee report, Goretti listened, as she attended to her newborn son. The names were many, and in a sing-song fashion they were read quickly but clearly. Suddenly Peter and Goretti looked at one another with astonishment. A five-year-old boy described with a facial scar and last named Kabuguza, just had to be their nephew Yannick! The radio announced the first name as Eric, but that had to be a mistake.

Goretti shook all over. "Could this be my sister's boy, Yannick?" she said.

Peter replied, "Let us not get our hopes up but we can go to the camp to see for ourselves."

They both wondered, that if they found Yannick, what it might do to their family dynamic but they had to find out to see if Yannick had, in fact, survived the genocide.

The radio refugee report ended with instructions that if anyone recognized the names, and wished to visit or claim one of the refugees, they should report to the camp administration office on Saturday morning for possible processing.

On a Saturday morning, sometime in the middle of April 1996, Yannick Kabuguza, a skinny five-year-old child with a nasty scar across his left cheek and a left ear nearly cut in half, trotted around the makeshift tents kicking a ball of plastic and pretending he was competing in a match against his campmates. Suddenly he heard his name called loudly. No one ever paid much attention to him usually but sure enough he heard his name a second time.

"Yannick, Yannick is that you?" he heard.

Could it be? He turned to see a woman he did not recognize. Goretti and Peter stood speechless for a moment. Then Goretti ran to Yannick and hugged him, the first hug he had received in over two years.

Goretti pulled back from Yannick and winced as she examined his face. *My God*, she thought to herself, *how could anyone do this to a child?* Beautiful Yannick's face was badly damaged and was still in need of medical care almost two whole years after he had been brutally attacked.

She hugged him again as Peter looked on silently.

Another mouth to feed, he thought. *How will we deal with this new responsibility?* He wondered. *I guess I have no choice but to welcome you, Yannick,* Peter thought to himself.

Goretti explained to Yannick that she was his mother's sister. He instantly believed her, because he saw a likeness of his mother in Goretti's eyes. He started to smile and cry at the same time. He hugged Goretti tightly while she whispered that he would be coming home with her.

"This is my husband, Peter, and you will live with us now," she said.

Even though Peter did not smile, Yannick thought, *This must be a dream, a miracle, I have a home? Maybe my sad nightmare is over? Maybe I will have a life?*

Goretti said to Yannick, "Come home boy, we will be your family now!"

A family, a home, my God I must be dreaming, Yannick thought, and ran to gather his makeshift soccer ball and some other pieces of clothing he acquired. Peter and Goretti looked at Yannick's clothes with disgust, for they were old dirty rags.

"Come, boy, now let us leave this horrible place," said Peter.

And off they went, to Yannick's amazement.

Finally, he thought, *I am saved!*

CHAPTER FIVE

The Storm Clouds Gather, Again

Yannick began to understand that his life was about to change so very drastically. His new reality would provide him a home with a real family, and an aunt and uncle who could be almost like a Mom and Dad to him. He walked into the house and could not stop smiling. Goretti showed Yannick his room and his very own bed where he would sleep in safety and security. He had a place that he could finally call his own. Goretti and Peter's home would be a place where he could store his own personal belongings, a little tiny area of the world that was his and his alone. He wept with tears of joy and could not believe that his prayers were answered. He was finally safe from the mean, hard world of the refugee camps and foster homes he had experienced. He lay down on his bed and cried until he had no more tears left, all the emotion drained from his body.

Maybe, he thought, *I can be a normal boy with a normal family and go to a normal school where I can learn and become an important respected person like my Grandpa Bosco.*

Just as he was about to fall asleep, to dream of a better life filled with joy, he heard his name called for only the third time in almost two years.

I must get used to this name because now I am a real boy with a real family who loves me, he thought.

"Yannick come here quick!" Goretti called his name again.

Yannick came out of his room and into the center of the house where Goretti and Peter stood.

"Come and see your cousin, Beradi," Goretti said.

Yannick looked to see a beautiful baby boy just about eight or nine months old. He was smiling at Yannick and babbling some words he didn't understand. Yannick immediately felt love again and he believed this little boy actually loved him back. Yannick looked at Beradi with peace, love, and joy, and desired to give him a hug. However, he wasn't sure of his role in the family yet and looked at Peter for approval. Peter nodded toward Yannick and then to Beradi signaling that it was okay to approach the baby boy.

Yannick held both of Beradi's hands and looked into his beautiful face and said, "Hello my cousin, it is nice to meet you."

Beradi opened his tiny mouth with a big smile and Yannick's heart leapt with delight. For the first time in forever, Yannick felt that someone could really love him no matter how his face looked or what his clothes looked like.

"This kid I will love forever no matter what," Yannick thought out loud.

Peter and Goretti watched Yannick from a distance letting the two boys get to know one another.

Goretti cooked a great big meal while Peter went outside to work on the yard.

Yannick spent time with Beradi watching his every move with fascination. After dinner was over and Yannick had filled his belly, Beradi was put to bed. Peter and Goretti spoke to Yannick very seriously for the very first time. They explained to Yannick that not only had his mother, grandfather and grandmother been killed, his father, step mom and four half siblings were slaughtered as well. Goretti explained to Yannick that she was, in fact, his only known surviving relative. She believed his cousins, including Penti, had survived but did not know where they were living.

Peter explained to Yannick that he would be welcomed in his home, but he would be expected to obey the rules of his household.

"I will provide for you a roof over your head and food enough to eat but you will behave yourself and do everything that we ask of you."

Yannick understood and thought, *As compared to where he lived, this would be a happy place for him.*

And at first it was. He had food to eat and a place to call his own. He had people who loved him, he thought, and a beautiful little boy cousin to have fun with when he grew up. *How bad could life be?* Yannick thought. This would be a walk in the park compared to what he'd been through. But sadly Yannick's dream home would slowly turn into his latest "nightmare." He just hadn't realized it yet.

Little by little the new mouth to feed and new presence of a nervous active little five-year-old boy became an ever-growing nuisance for Peter. He became short tempered with him and often yelled and shouted at Yannick. When Peter's friends and neighbors would come to visit, Peter shooed Yannick back into his room like a misbehaved dog. The truth was, Peter would admit later, he was ashamed of Yannick and his ever-present scar on his face and ear. His very existence was a constant reminder of the genocide and the many friends and family members Peter and Goretti had lost—a reminder of the times they had tried to block out. Whenever they looked at Yannick they had little choice but to have vivid, horrible memories come rushing back.

As time moved on, resentment grew. Peter's bitterness toward Yannick heightened whenever he drank alcohol, and he would turn nasty and violent. Sometimes, Peter would beat Yannick when he was drunk for no good reason. Goretti tried to protect Yannick from Peter's wrath, but she would risk being beaten herself if she interfered too much. She was helpless to help Yannick when Peter was in one of his violent moods.

When Goretti gave birth to her second child, Tracy, a baby girl, Yannick's duties doubled. Not only was Yannick now seven years-old and required and expected to care for Beradi, he was now expected to look after Tracy as well. Yannick's duties included feeding the children, changing their diapers, keeping them and the house clean. All the while Yannick knew to stay out of sight and sound of Peter as much as he possibly could.

Yannick never complained about caring for Beradi and Tracy. He loved them. He learned to care for their every need and even helped them get well when they were sick. As they grew older, Yannick loved to teach them new words and tell them stories he had overheard.

Yannick slowly became more of a house servant than a part of Peter and Goretti's family. He learned to do his chores and care for his young cousins or face being beaten by Peter.

Yannick also learned not to be a burden to the family or make any mess. This was a lesson he learned one day when he wet his bed at the age of eight. After Peter discovered that Yannick had wet his mattress he screamed at Yannick that he was a filthy little boy and wasn't worthy of his generosity or of living in his house. Peter worked himself into such a violent rage that he took the wire cord from the house radio and whipped the back of Yannick's legs and backside until Yannick had welts all over his lower body and blood was coming from the backs of his knees. The stinging of the wire was almost unbearable.

Yannick tried to make no sound for fear that the beating would get worse.

The best moments Yannick had in the house were when both Goretti and Peter were out and Yannick was able to take care of Beradi and Tracy on his own. He loved to play with them and teach them all he knew.

They loved Yannick as well and would look to him for kindness and support, sometimes even more than they would from their own mother and father. As difficult as Yannick's life grew with Peter and Goretti, Yannick always felt very close to his young cousins. The kids gave him reason to live. He loved them and they loved him in return.

When Beradi and Tracy were old enough to attend school, it was Yannick's job to get them dressed, fed, and to school on time—all of which he was ordered to do or face the beatings of Peter. Yannick was unable to attend school himself until Beradi and Tracy were brought to their school. For years he would get the children situated in their school, help them with their studies, and stay at home with them if they were ill.

It was understood that only after Beradi and Tracy were cared for that Yannick could even begin to think of attending school on his own.

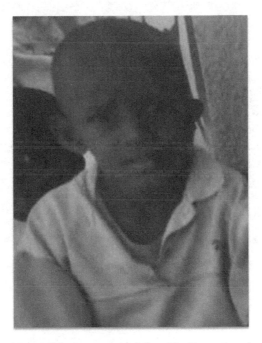

Yannick begins a new life with Goretti and Peter

The beautiful children of Rwanda

CHAPTER SIX

What Doesn't Kill You Makes You Stronger

As the years dragged on, Yannick lived up to his end of the bargain. He cooked, cleaned, washed and cared for his cousins' every need. For his work, he was fed and housed but given little else in the way of his care or needs. He felt unloved, with the exception, of course, of the mutual love he felt from and toward Beradi and Tracy. However, there were times both children took Yannick for granted and ordered him around as if he were their servant. They learned this behavior from watching their Mom and Dad treat Yannick like he was somehow less important or inferior to them.

When parties were held outside the home, Yannick was never invited. When parties were held at Goretti and Peter's home and company was present, Yannick was banished to his room and told to keep himself and his ugly scar away from guests.

Whenever Yannick had the chance, he would grab the homemade soccer ball from his closet and run outside with it. He loved his freedom to play whenever possible. Rarely was anyone around to play with him. Many times when children his own age were at school he was left home alone to run errands or do chores, so he would steal time with his ball and run with a free spirit. The joy he found with his soccer ball he could find with nothing else.

He became very skilled at controlling the ball, the speed of it, and the balance of it. He could carry it on his head, neck and knees. He would flick it from the instep of his foot to his head and back again without even looking at it. As the years went on, Yannick handled a soccer ball as if he had a string attached to it. He could make it do almost anything he willed it to do instinctively and without a second thought. Peter would yell at Yannick if he played too much soccer and thought it was a waste of time when he could be cleaning or working around the house, using his time for more productive endeavors. But it was Yannick's passion and for him it was a feeling of freedom. It was proof that he at least possessed some skill.

As Beradi and Tracy got older they became more independent of Yannick, and that left more time for Yannick to attend school more frequently. By the time Yannick turned 13 he was in school almost regularly but all the missed schooling had delayed his advancement and his education. Despite Yannick showing remarkable intellect, he could not make up for all of the time he had lost while caring for Beradi and Tracy all those years.

Yannick plodded along in his classes trying to learn and catch up with the other children his age. But it proved quite difficult. Rwandan teachers would routinely beat their students for not having the questions correct.

With that being said, Yannick received more than his fair share of teacher beatings, smacks and punches to the back of his head, and cracks of rulers on his hands were, unfortunately, quite common. His scar, of course, was ever present and it continued to cause harassment and ridicule from both teachers and his fellow students.

One student in particular would mock and tease Yannick daily. His name, ironically, was Christian. Christian was a slightly bigger kid than Yannick, and he delighted at tormenting Yannick.

Christian constantly teased Yannick saying, "You must've been a thief and got caught by the military authorities and that is why your face is disfigured."

This caused Yannick great humiliation, but he refused to retaliate or fight back. He kept to himself mostly because he was deeply saddened by the teasing of Christian and many others. There was, however, one wonderful young man named Maradona, after the famous Argentinian soccer star, who was a hero to Yannick. Maradona was very strong, good-looking and very popular with everyone. He protected Yannick and stuck up for him when anyone would tease him. He felt sorry for Yannick and threatened to beat up anyone who was mean to him. Sadly though, when Maradona was not around Christian and others would resume their torment of the boy with the ugly scar on his face.

Yannick's best memories of his school days were when he played on the soccer field for his school against other teams. He dominated play and scored many goals and at least for those moments he felt like a part of something.

Other than that, Yannick was growing more and more depressed.

There was one teacher who took pity on Yannick. Her name was Mary. Teacher Mary always favored Yannick. In fact, Mary favored Yannick so much she would never reprimand or beat him when he made a mistake or answered incorrectly. While she beat the other students in Yannick's class, she would never touch Yannick. The other children began to notice and this caused even more of a problem for Yannick. They called him the teachers' pet and ridiculed him. Christian was especially hard on Yannick for this. Yannick actually had to ask teacher Mary to please beat him in front of the other students, so that Yannick might be left alone. Mary could not believe his request but complied to help Yannick any way she could even though she felt terrible about it.

Yannick had reached a point in his life when he had so many unanswered questions. *Why had God spared him? Why couldn't he be like all the other kids with a normal face and a normal family? Why wasn't he allowed to go to school on time? Why was he put in charge of the children and what made them better than him?*

He was extremely depressed and wondered if life was even worth living. Day after day, Yannick struggled for reasons to keep going. He felt worthless at times and turned to smoking a form of marijuana called "Banana Weed" to try to ease his mind. It was an extremely low point in his life.

He came to school one day and sat, as he always did, in the back of the room and prepared his notes for another boring day of school. Just then the principal walked into the room and Teacher Mary called the class to order, requested silence, and demanded absolute attention be given to the principal and the athletic director of the school. The principal announced that he had wonderful news to share with the class. He announced that their school had won the county soccer championship and that one of their classmates was voted the most outstanding player for the entire year. Yannick sat up straight and listened intently. He almost could not believe his ears as the principal continued, "In an incredible display of athletic ability for scoring the most goals in the entire tournament, our very own Yannick Kabuguza has been voted this year's 'Most Outstanding Player!'"

The class exploded with applause and cheers. Every student turned toward Yannick with disbelief, smiled and rose to their feet. The cheering and clapping was so loud Yannick could only blush and smile and sheepishly lower his head. But the cheering only grew louder as the principal called Yannick to the front of the room. The principal and Teacher Mary handed Yannick a silver cup trophy.

"I must tell you all, I saw some of these games and witnessed Yannick's play, and Yannick is number one in my book!" the principal declared.

The entire class began to chant loudly, "Mr. Number One, Mr. Number One, Mr. Number One!"

Yannick smiled and felt like the happiest young man on the face of the earth. All day he kept his big smile on his face, through recess and after school.

The other students patted Yannick on the back and said, "Way to go Mr. Number One, you should be proud."

Another student said, "Congratulations on such a remarkable achievement and bringing great honor to our school."

What a wonderful day it had been for Yannick. He almost floated home as if on a cloud. When he told Goretti, Peter, Beradi and Tracy they all smiled and congratulated him. Even Peter was so much nicer to Yannick that night. As Yannick lay in his bed and stared at the ceiling smiling, he thought, *Finally, I am worth something.* He felt special in a good way this time for the first time in his life. He thought, *Maybe I am worth more than I thought and maybe I finally might have a life worth living.*

Brian Dolaghan and Jean Paul display a homemade soccer ball

Rwandan farmers harvest their Tea

CHAPTER SEVEN

My Time To Learn

To say that being honored with the soccer trophy and earning the nickname "Mr. Number One" changed Yannick's life would be a gross understatement.

The next two years were not that much better for Yannick at home. He still had all the same tedious chores. He still had the feeling of being less than a full member of the family. He was still treated with little or no respect. He still suffered the drunken beatings and rants from Peter, some actually more violent and brutal than ever. But somehow Yannick was now able to handle his hardships with more strength, courage and hope. He studied with more purpose and his thirst for more knowledge and better grades increased. He was more focused and more confident.

Yannick was treated better, at least at school, and his body grew stronger as he exercised with more fervor. Even though his life was still quite difficult, he now had the feeling that this hardship would not be forever. As Mr. Number One, he could now dream with more hope in his heart because he had proven to himself and others that he was special somehow. Not special in the way that he had felt in association with his genocide facial scar, but special in an exceptionally good way, a skilled way, a brilliant way. In many ways, on the day of his award when he became Mr. Number One, a fire was lit within him that he felt would never be extinguished. No matter who mocked him or beat him or disrespected him, he now knew in his own mind and heart he was spared by God for a reason.

Yannick now believed he was not meant to remain a victim but rather to be a triumph, something good, bigger than he was even able to imagine. But Yannick did not know what or how he would climb from the depths of despair, poverty and discrimination due to his disfigurement. He just believed in himself now in a way he couldn't explain or even understand.

By the time Yannick turned 15 he was almost six feet tall and getting stronger and running faster. He began to learn the game of basketball and enjoyed playing with his classmates. He started to have more and more friends who respected him for his strength and athletics. Girls did not pay much attention yet to Yannick and, in turn, he had little or no interest in them. Despite his poor home life, he was getting very good grades now and learning and loving his language skills. His friends gained respect for Yannick's dedication to fitness and his knowledge and intellect. His confidence was starting to build and hope was in his heart and mind.

Right around the time Yannick was gaining in confidence and learning to accept his plight and occasional beating at the hands of his drunken uncle Peter, Yannick got another boost of good fortune. His cousins, Maurice and Aimee, came to visit Yannick that fall. Maurice and Aimee were almost 10 years older than Yannick.

They too had lost their parents in the genocide. Their brothers and sisters (five in total) were all separated and sent to different foster families.

Maurice had been adopted by a French family who were quite well to do. Maurice had not only survived in France but had attained a good education in film making, and had been living a life of affluence with his adopted family. While Aimee's foster family was not as wealthy as the family who adopted Maurice, she too had the benefit of a happy home. Maurice and Aimee worked constantly to reunite with their brothers and sisters. Now they were thrilled to have found their cousin Yannick and wanted to help him. Yannick was thrilled to learn that all his cousins had survived the genocide, especially his former fake-soldier playmate, Penti.

Maurice explained to Yannick that Penti was doing well and living with a fine family in the countryside. Maurice assisted Yannick with advice and money. Maurice also provided better clothing and basketball sneakers and some electronics for Yannick. Aimee provided counsel and encouragement that was so vital to Yannick at this time of his life. Yannick grew to respect and love both Aimee and Maurice, as they proved so kind and caring unlike he had ever known.

It did not take Maurice and Aimee long to witness the home life Yannick was suffering. Goretti was the sister of Maurice and Aimee's mom, and they loved her as their aunt. What they continued to witness, however, was a dysfunctional household that placed their cousin in an abusive environment. They could not allow it to continue.

Maurice was a steady, positive influence on Yannick at just the time Yannick needed him most. Aimee would also look out for Yannick and give him the female nurturing he was unable to get from Goretti due to the negative overbearing presence of Peter and his alcoholism.

Maurice insisted that Yannick leave the household and find a better living environment. Despite Yannick being in favor of making a change, he was somewhat torn about leaving Beradi and Tracy. He had been almost like a father to them, and he loved them dearly. And, of course, despite not always treating Yannick with respect, Beradi and Tracy loved their older cousin very deeply and secretly respected his efforts on their behalf very, very much.

Although Beradi, Tracy and Goretti were sad that Yannick would be leaving the house, they knew Yannick needed his independence and a more stable living space of his own. Peter, on the other hand, could not understand Yannick's decision and viewed his leaving as a act of ungratefulness and a sort of betrayal. Isn't it quite amazing how alcohol can blur an individual's reality? Peter at the time had little or no understanding of exactly how abusive and cruel he had been to Yannick for the duration of Yannick's time living with them. When Maurice helped Yannick move out of Peter and Goretti's house, it ended a decade of humiliation and abuse for Yannick. This day felt like an emancipation day from servitude for Yannick and would be the beginning of the rest of his life.

Maurice and Aimee found a place for Yannick to live with an older Kigali woman named Speciose who he instantly grew to love, and referred to as "Grandma". Speciose welcomed Yannick into her home with love and affection. Yannick was not used to that kind of treatment. He never realized a person could be so caring, kind, and attentive to his every need. Instead of Yannick having to do all the chores of the house, Speciose cooked his favorite foods, cleaned his clothes, and showed Yannick the familial love he longed to experience. Since the days his mother and grandparents were killed, Yannick had not felt this amazing feeling of being wanted and valued. Yannick's stay with Grandma Speciose translated into a happier Yannick, a more confident Yannick, and a more expressive and social Yannick. His grades improved and he focused on learning all that he could to enhance his knowledge. His dreams of success grew bigger, and he valued himself more than he ever could have imagined.

Basketball, soccer, reading, and schoolwork and an occasional party with friends filled the later teen years for Yannick into his twenties. Yannick kept more and more in touch with Maurice and Aimee, and their influence on him continued to do wonders. In fact at times Yannick become so confident that he almost forgot about his scar. But then again, there was always some insensitive or ignorant soul to remind Yannick of the mark of the genocide he carried with him every day of his life.

It wasn't until the age of 23 that Yannick had earned the amount of educational credits to graduate high school. The hardships imposed on him by Peter and Goretti, and the sacrifice Yannick made on behalf of Beradi and Tracy, had cost Yannick so many vital years of his youth and delayed his education significantly. It was only because of Yannick's superior intellect and perseverance that he was able to graduate and earn his high school diploma.

His graduation, regardless of his age, was a great cause of celebration for him. Grandma Speciose, Maurice and Aimee all congratulated Yannick and were quite proud of this young man.

Yannick earned the respect of all of his friends for never letting his hardships or obstacles prevent him from achieving his goal to graduate. This determination would be the latest sign that Yannick was determined to be someone great and, against all odds would be a success.

A bicycle serving Rwandan commerce

CHAPTER EIGHT

Forgive to Survive

After graduating high school, Yannick found a job as a security guard with the KK Security Company. His job was to watch over their buildings and office spaces. Yannick later became the security officer for the World Food Program. He proved to be hardworking, reliable and always punctual. He prided himself on wearing a very neat uniform, always pressed and clean.

In addition to the security job, Yannick worked as a delivery driver for the BMS Construction Company where he delivered supplies and helped with the loading and unloading of materials. Neither job paid very much, only a few American dollars a week. Yannick knew his life would not change in the way he dreamt if he continued with his current employment for very long.

On his off time, Yannick enjoyed his social life with friends. He liked an occasional smoke of marijuana because he believed that and some beer were the only things that gave him some temporary relief from the pain his facial wound created. The vision in his left eye was now beginning to be impacted due to the ever-present scar and the fact it had never really healed properly or was never attended to medically the way it should have been.

Marijuana, which was illegal throughout Rwanda, served its purpose, although occasionally causing him trouble with the local police. Yannick was really a hard worker and solid citizen but his self-medication habit did cause an occasional arrest from time to time. These visits to the jail were extremely unpleasant as all types of criminals were thrown together in one large jail cell. This served as a great deterrent for Yannick and he steered clear of any more trouble with the law.

Such was Yannick's life at the age of 24. He worked, played sports, partied with his friends, spent time with Grandma Speciose, kept a clean home and repeated the ritual day after day. Yannick spent more and more time with Aimee and her children Sacha and Amariza. He felt a strong connection to these children and loved being thought of as part of another family. Aimee continued to influence Yannick and made him imagine a bright future and to dream of having a family of his own one day.

Yannick was at an age now when he desired to know more about what had happened to him. There were so many unanswered questions about how he had survived and what happened to the people who had hurt him as well as those who saved him. Maurice was a great resource for Yannick, helping him to fill in the blank spaces of his shattered memories. When Maurice was able to locate Karigo, the neighbor who saved Yannick and nursed him back to health, an emotional reunion was arranged. Yannick owed Karigo his life but Karigo carried strong feelings of personal guilt for having left Yannick at the bus stop more than twenty years ago.

Karigo was thrilled to learn that Yannick had survived. She was very nervous about seeing him again until Yannick greeted her with the biggest hug and embraced her as his savior. Yannick and Karigo spoke often and became very close in the months to come, each one consoling the other as they navigated their respective painful memories. Yannick was trying to understand how people could be so cruel to one another. He asked specifically about his neighbor, Kayibanda. He wanted to know why he had turned on him and hurt him so terribly, and why he changed his mind about killing him.

How could people commit such horrible crimes? Yannick wondered.

Karigo was able to find out where Kayibanda was imprisoned. Yannick wanted to confront him and ask him why and how he could commit such crimes.

This man had been a friend of the family, and yet he joined the crazed Hutu soldiers. Kayibanda was, in fact, a Tutsi, which made it even more difficult for Yannick to understand his actions.

Yannick mustered the courage to visit the prison and confront his attacker. Kayibanda was mortified to meet Yannick after he realized who this young man was and remembered what he had done to him. The shame was too much for Kayibanda to handle. He wept and covered his face, unable to look Yannick in the eye. But something miraculous happened at that meeting.

Yannick actually took pity on Kayibanda and comforted him. Kayibanda tearfully confessed that he joined the enemy Hutu soldiers out of fear for his own life and that he was a coward and ashamed of what he had done.

Kayibanda also told Yannick he was so sorry for everything he had done and lived in a mental and emotional prison because of his weakness. Yannick was moved to tears as well and was compelled to tell Kayibanda that he forgave him and that everything would be ok. Kayibanda could not believe Yannick's kindness and remarkable gift of forgiveness and turned away and wept bitterly.

That day, after visiting Kayibanda, Yannick felt like a great weight had been lifted from him. He felt light and close to God. This man had hurt him and been involved with the destruction of his life and all of his loved ones. Yet Yannick realized Kayibanda also was suffering for his crimes and cowardice. Forgiving Kayibanda and the rest of the war criminals who killed his family was Yannick's gift not to them but to himself. The visit and ultimate forgiving of Kayibanda changed Yannick forever. He felt free and able to put the past behind him and now felt a new energy to start an unencumbered life. Yannick continued to visit Kayibanda in prison and even brought him money to help make his life a little easier. Yannick's actions, while hard to comprehend, underscore the spiritual change that Yannick now enjoyed. His story is an incredible example of love and kindness in the face of evil and wickedness, was starting to resonate with other Rwandans. He now felt free and renewed and prepared to take on the world and make something of himself.

One day, Maurice asked Yannick if he would like to come and work on a film project with him. Maurice explained that he had met an

American doctor who had become a student at the film school where Maurice taught. His name was Dr. Jim Creighton. Dr. Jim had just completed his career as a medical doctor with the Peace Corps and was starting a film company called AKAGERA Productions, named after the Rwandan National Park.

Dr. Jim was learning the film business and was interested in producing documentaries of all types and subjects pertaining to Rwanda and its culture.

Yannick jumped at the chance to work with Maurice, and he soon joined the team at AKAGERA Productions. Another new chapter of his life was launched.

Dr. Jim Creighton was quite the Renaissance man. He had been a medical doctor with the Peace Corp for over twenty years in developing countries all across Africa. He was a big-hearted humanitarian who had dedicated his life to saving others and bringing modern medicine to the far reaches and remotest places on earth.

Dr. Jim was as brilliant as he was generous of spirit. Dr. Jim not only had a medical degree but a law degree and Masters in Business as well.

After his retirement from medicine he decided to use the other side of his brain and try his hand at filmmaking. Film school is where he met Maurice and ultimately how he came to know Yannick.

Yannick joined the AKAGERA Productions team and was immediately welcomed with open arms. Dr. Jim took an instant liking to Yannick. His medical training led him to care for and assess Yannick's ear and facial scar in a way that previously had not been done. Dr. Jim began to formulate a plan to try and repair his face and his ear in an attempt to improve Yannick's quality of life.

Besides the close relationship Yannick was soon to build with Dr. Jim, he also had an ally in Gene MacDonald, Jim's wife. Gene held a Ph.D in immunology and microbiology. She was the current Country Director of the CDC for Rwanda. A brilliant woman with a heart to match, Gene immediately took a strong liking to Yannick.

Yannick would often joke with Jim and Gene as to who was the smarter of the two. Dr. Jim would of course say Gene was—hands down—and Gene would quickly remind everyone that while she had to study to earn her degrees, knowledge came quite easily to Dr. Jim and that he was naturally the smarter of the two. Overly humble, brilliant and remarkable people they were a perfect match for one another. Yannick could hardly believe his good fortune of being around these two exceptional human beings.

Jim and Gene treated Yannick like family from the start. They welcomed him into not only the AKAGERA Company, but included him with their children, Sean, who was fourteen at the time, and their beautiful twin girls, Caroline and Palesa, who were thirteen. Sean was a precocious lad, a child genius really smart beyond his years and the girls were sweet, caring, and brilliant as well, but with a softer artistic and creative kind of intellect.

They all treated Yannick quite well and Sean especially socialized with Yannick as kind of a big brother. They all showed Yannick respect, kindness and generosity.

Dr. Jim was building his film crew with talented Rwandan locals with the advice from Maurice, who seemed to have a great network and an eye for talented and industrious workers. There was Robert who was a soft-spoken, deep thinker and clever fellow, who knew his way around a camera and was studying sound. Dixon and Charles were two strong, smart young men who Yannick instantly liked.

They exhibited a raw talent and were quick learners. Dr. Jim rented a small house that he turned into a studio and set for the show, *Mutoni* that he was producing. *Mutoni* was a Rwandan sitcom with an underlying health care message to educate the young Rwandan population. Yannick, Maurice, Robert, Charles and Dixon all worked together on this ambitious project and got along quite well.

It wasn't long before Yannick was living with Dixon, Charles, Robert and Maurice in the studio where they could work long hours and live together as a cohesive team.

What an opportunity this was for Yannick. He began his career at AKAGERA as a utility man, sort of a "jack -of -all -trades." He would run errands for the others and filled in when and wherever he was needed. Yannick learned more and more English as he spent time with his new comrades. Like a sponge, he soaked up as much knowledge of the business in all sorts of subjects and became more and more fascinated with the United States of America which was where Dr. Jim and Gene had grown up and received most of their remarkable and extensive education. Yannick immediately recognized that this work opportunity was so much more than a job. It was a gift from God and pathway out of poverty and mediocrity to greater possibilities, that is, if he was smart and disciplined enough to take full advantage!

Once again, Maurice had been a blessing to Yannick and set him up for the success of which he might be capable. It would take hard work and perseverance but he believed in himself and was ready to give it all that he had inside.

* * *

End of Part I

CHAPTER NINE

Where Angels Play Foundation Background

Just about the time Yannick Kabuguza was completing his high school education in Kigali, Rwanda, 7,000 miles away, across the vast Atlantic Ocean in Woodbridge, New Jersey, the Where Angels Play Foundation was being formed.

It was late December 2012 and an organization of New Jersey Firefighters known as the New Jersey Firefighters Mutual Benevolent Association (NJFMBA) began to lay the groundwork for what would ultimately be called the Where Angels Play Foundation.

Many members of the NJFMBA had responded to the World Trade Center attack on September 11, 2001. That day and subsequent aftermath would serve as the worst period of time in the history of the modern fire service. All firefighters would struggle—physically, emotionally, spiritually and socially—to process the gravity and grief of what happened in New York City that fateful day.

New Jersey Firefighters who would support their brother firefighters from the Fire Department of New York (FDNY), suffered right along with their brothers and sisters across the Hudson River. Many charitable and supportive campaigns were borne out of the historic tragedy of 9/11.

In early October 2001, the Elizabeth Fire Department received a large mailbox full of cards and letters from a third grade class from the North Bay Elementary School in Bay Saint Louis, Mississippi. This third grade class, was taught by a wonderful, compassionate and enthusiastic teacher, Jackie Wintruba. Ms. Wintruba asked her students to write expressions of hope and support to the firefighters. Jackie was directed to forward the letters to Elizabeth Fire Chief Louis Kelly by her fellow teacher, Colleen Rice Hodge, the niece of Fire Captain Jay Rice, also from Elizabeth and sent the letters to them. The letters and mailbox were displayed at the new Elizabeth Fire Headquarters for the next several years.

These expressions of support from youngsters, so far away, buoyed the spirits of the members of the Elizabeth Fire Department.

Four years later, the worst storm in over a hundred years hit the United States, Hurricane Katrina, devastating the Gulf Coast and, in doing so, destroyed the North Bay Elementary School. The Elizabeth Firefighters and the leadership of their labor union, the New Jersey Firefighters Mutual Benevolent Association, wondered what had happened to the kind and caring children who had sent those letters of encouragement and support in the wake of 9/11.

Finding out about the complete destruction of the area and in particular, the North Bay Elementary School, the NJFMBA, with the help of United States Senator Jon Corzine, raised over $400,000 and sent that donation to Save the Children designating that money for support of the children of the Gulf Coast. Six months later, Save the Children invited members of the NJFMBA to visit the devastation caused by Hurricane Katrina and witness the great work being done for the children of the Gulf with the money the firefighters had contributed.

Upon seeing the debris and total destruction on such a large scale, as well as the lack of resources for children's recreation, it was agreed that the firefighters would come back to the area and build a playground for the kids of North Bay Elementary School as their playground had been destroyed. So as a "pay it forward" gesture, the NJFMBA built, not one but three of the first fully handicapped-accessible playgrounds in the State of Mississippi and the Gulf area. This endeavor became a most rewarding experience and far beyond the firefighters wildest dreams.

Seven years later the same New Jersey firefighters were experiencing a devastating storm of their own. On October 29, 2012, Super

Storm Sandy flooded and destroyed a large portion of the coastline of New York, New Jersey and Connecticut.

Just as the NJFMBA began to help with the rebuilding and restoring of their coastline in New Jersey, the worst school shooting in American history shattered the innocent, sleepy town of Newtown, Connecticut. Twenty beautiful young children and six courageous and inspiring educators were massacred at the Sandy Hook Elementary School.

The tragedy at Sandy Hook impacted the firefighters so very much that all of their recovery efforts came to a screeching halt. That is until a video email message was sent to the president of the NJFMBA, Bill Lavin. The same 3rd grade class from North Bay Elementary School gave birth to a wonderful idea. The message simply thanked the New Jersey firefighters for the playground they had built for them in Mississippi, and as a "pay it forward" gesture, the children of the Gulf had collected Christmas gifts for the children of New Jersey who were impacted by Super Storm Sandy.

Thousands of gifts from the people of the Gulf Coast and the students of the rebuilt North Bay Elementary School would eventually reach the shores of New Jersey and be placed under the Christmas trees of needy New Jersey children on Christmas morning.

Even more remarkable than the gifts, were the words spoken on that video by 10-year-old Carly Coyne. Carly, a third grade student, spoke about the playground on which she loved to play. Carly's words of gratitude inspired the idea to build playgrounds for each one of the victims of Sandy Hook Elementary School shooting.

Bill Lavin would reach out to all the families from Sandy Hook to see if they would be interested in a playground to celebrate the life of their loved one, affectionately referred to as their Angel. Eventually all 26 families would trust them with the memory of their Angel and the Where Angels Play Foundation had officially begun.

The playgrounds were built with grassroots support from volunteers, primarily made up of the New Jersey Fire Service and professional expertise of Picerno/Giordano Contractors led by Toni and Rich Picerno. The families would design and build the playgrounds alongside the Where Angels Play Foundation, whose volunteers self-named themselves the "Angels Army." In a matter of 19 months, after raising 3 million dollars, the foundation had completed all 26 playgrounds for the greatest families they could ever meet and in the most welcoming communities they could have ever chosen. Most of those communities were seriously impacted by the Super Storm Sandy natural disaster. Communities benefitted from a brand new fully handicapped-accessible playground while wrapping their collective arms around a family in great need of healing, joy and support. The spirit of the Angel and the courage and strength of the Angels' family would serve as an incredible inspiration and living example of resiliency for everyone involved.

In the years to come the Where Angels Play Foundation would become an incredible charitable movement that reached thousands of people. The network of volunteers continued to grow with each playground and community project.

The entire story of Where Angels Play Foundation can be found in the prequel to this book entitled, *Where Angels Live, Work and Play* written by William and Smitty Lavin.

The momentum of healing and recovery would inspire the volunteers of the Where Angels Play Foundation to continue to build playgrounds for other needy communities and deserving families across the United States of America, Canada and Puerto Rico. Where Angels Play Foundation was eventually led to Kibeho, Rwanda and that beautiful location provides the backdrop and the inspiration for the story of the *Starfish from Africa*.

PART II

Triumph

Written in the first person by Bill Lavin

"To forgive is to set a prisoner free and discover that prisoner was you."

— *Lewis B. Smedes*

The New Colossus

By Emma Lazarus

Not like the brazen giant of Greek fame,
With conquering limbs astride from land to land;
Here at our sea-washed, sunset gates shall stand
A mighty woman with a torch, whose flame
Is the imprisoned lightning, and her name
Mother of Exiles. From her beacon-hand
Glows world-wide welcome; her mild eyes command
The air-bridged harbor that twin cities frame.
"Keep, ancient lands, your storied pomp!" cries she
With silent lips. "Give me your tired, your poor,
Your huddled masses yearning to breathe free,
The wretched refuse of your teeming shore.
Send these, the homeless, tempest-tost to me,
I lift my lamp beside the golden door!"

CHAPTER TEN

From Newtown to Rwanda

The experience of the Where Angels Play Foundation and all its volunteers was a blessing and a gift to every one of us who have had the privilege to play even a small part. I can speak for my family and so many others that the greatest blessing we received from the foundation was the honor of meeting, getting to know and falling in love with the families of the Sandy Hook Elementary School Angels. This sentiment also extends to the families of every Angel we had the honor to celebrate with a playground. Each family, special in their own right, is a relationship and a memory we will treasure for a lifetime.

Scarlett Lewis is the mother of Sandy Hook Elementary School hero and Angel, Jesse Lewis. Scarlett became an integral part of the "Angels Army" and after getting to know her and Jesse and surviving son J.T. as well as her mom, Maureen, and stepdad Bob, we considered them all family. Scarlett has a special spirit about her and her insight, philosophy and wisdom are changing the world through her work at the Jesse Lewis Choose Love Foundation.

In the aftermath of the tragic Sandy Hook School shooting, Scarlett Lewis and her son J.T. were working through their grief with counselors. Scarlet was making progress and was beginning to heal, but J.T. remained withdrawn, angry and had no interest in attending school. One of Scarlett's grief counselors suggested to Scarlett that she connect J.T. with a wonderful Rwandan Genocide Survivor, eighteen-year old student, Chantal. Chantal had survived the genocide in her country and it was believed she might be a great resource to help J.T. process his anger and grief.

Chantal, who had lost her entire family and most of her village, counseled J.T. so remarkably well, that J.T. not only went back to school, he created a foundation called Newtown for Rwanda in an effort to repay Chantal for her kindness. J.T.'s foundation would serve to provide educational scholarships for Chantal and many other students from Rwanda.

Not long after hearing that story from Scarlett, I was contacted by a group from the Chicago area called Kids Around the World. They had seen the story of the Where Angels Play Foundation on the internet and wondered whether we might consider building a playground somewhere outside of the country in partnership with them.

It sounded like an exciting possibility, and I immediately thought of the country of Rwanda, a place that I had rarely heard about and knew almost nothing except for the amazing story of J.T.'s inspiration and the support offered by the young Rwandan, Chantal.

When I suggested Rwanda as a possible location for a playground build, the folks from Kids Around the World replied, "Why not! I'm sure they could use a playground as much as anybody else."

When I reached out to Scarlett Lewis about the idea to build a playground in the country of Rwanda as a "pay it forward" response to Chantal's efforts, Scarlett immediately loved the idea and offered any and all help that she could possibly give.

Scarlett had made some contacts in Rwanda for us and had a perfect location for a playground at a needy school in Kibeho, Rwanda. We began to discuss the logistics, and connections were made in Kibeho for a possible playground sometime in the near future.

Tony Wieners, my great friend and fellow labor leader, had traveled overseas recently with Habitat for Humanity and had agreed to take the trip with me to explore the country of Rwanda and the village of Kibeho.

In late November, 2016, Tony and I flew the eighteen hours to Kigali, Rwanda, where we met up with a group of American tourists who were on a pilgrimage to the village of Kibeho. Kibeho was famous because the Blessed Mother had appeared to young teenage girls back in 1981, foretelling the genocide that would eventually take place in 1994.

Tony and I traveled with the religious pilgrims and were impressed by their devotion and strong belief. We stayed at a Catholic retreat house in Kibeho and met with some government and religious leaders. These members of the clergy we hoped would help us procure the building materials necessary for a playground installation. We visited the Mother of the Word School which would be the beneficiary of our project and met some of the nuns there. The school was in great need of repair and had horrible sanitation systems with very little in the way of plumbing. Seeing the sad faces of the children who needed just about everything was an image that became etched in our mind.

As dire a situation that faced the children of the Mother of the Word School, it paled in comparison to the quality of life the people faced outside of its walls. Hunger was evident in most places. The villagers' clothes were no more than rags. There was no electricity or running water in most places. People washed themselves and their clothes in brown, muddy water rivers. The roads were almost non-existent. Bridges meant to navigate creeks and rivers were no more than felled trees that were spaced across the river. Our bus had to line up its tires perfectly to travel across it. Food was scarce and the quality of life was so obviously difficult. It was clear these children needed our help and we could definitely make a difference for at least some of this community.

Tony and I decided that we must return and deliver a playground where they had never seen one. The Rwandan people left an impression on me that remains with me to this day. Despite needing everything, they smiled and were polite. They seemed happy although they had almost nothing in comparison to the poorest American child.

Tony remarked, "Prisoners on death row in the U.S. have a better quality of life than these poor Rwandan folks."

So we left the Catholic pilgrims with an education about "Our Lady of Kibeho" and witnessed the incredible faith of the Rwandan people. Africans from surrounding countries of Kenya, Democratic

Republic of the Congo, Tanzania and Burundi had walked hundreds of miles to attend the feast day of "Our Lady of Kibeho" on November 28th. Tony and I attended the Mass on the day of the feast.

It'd be hard for me to guess, but conservatively 30,000 people attended the vigil and Mass that followed. One irony that was etched in my mind was the offertory procession. The poorest people on earth were lining up to give the priests anything and everything they could spare. Rice, vegetables, mops, squeegees, garments, arts and crafts—anything of value that they could find in their homes to honor the church and the Blessed Mother. I couldn't help but think, *shouldn't it be the other way around?* The priests and bishops appeared to be well fed, well groomed and lived a comfortable life. My take away was that a vocation to the church was, for some, a path out of abject poverty.

As Tony and I left our new friends we vowed to return and that the next time we would do all we could to bring some much needed joy to these beautiful but greatly challenged people.

The decision to travel to East Africa was not an easy one for Where Angels Play. As of the fall of 2018, all of the playgrounds we had built were within only a couple hundred miles of our home base of New Jersey on the continent of North America. Our volunteers could all travel to these locations by car or a short flight. This project was another matter all together. The commitment of the "Angels Army" and all the volunteers that supported each playground build was overwhelming. Never before had I witnessed in all my life the willingness of so many complete strangers to rally together and advocate for a family or a community in need.

Volunteers were asked to work in all kinds of weather to which they were not accustomed, travel long distances at their own expense, and complete labor-intensive tasks. Volunteers were asked to spend time away from their families and work together with strangers all in an effort to do the impossible. That impossible task was to soften the grief and attempt to begin to heal moms, dads, sisters, brothers, grandmas and grandpas and all who had suffered the greatest loss of a loved one.

Sometimes that tragic loss was due to violence, a disease, illness or sometimes a horrific accident. It didn't matter.

Playgrounds were built for police officers, firefighters, teachers, and administrators, but mostly the playgrounds of the Where Angels Play Foundation were dedicated to children.

The ambitious idea to build a playground 7,000 miles away in East Africa was celebrated by some—rejected by others. Could the Where Angels Play Foundation safely travel to Rwanda, a country that had a violent history of civil war and genocide? As the founder of the Where Angels Play Foundation, I vowed to always listen to the Angels and try and to be open to where they might lead us. We speak often of the countless signs the Angels leave us, and I truly believe that it is the beautiful spirits of these children who are ultimately in charge of our foundation and where and how we should operate. I felt a strong calling to Africa through Jesse Lewis, the child of Scarlett and the grandson of Maureen.

I also felt an obligation to listen to my fellow volunteers. Many would be prohibited from traveling to Rwanda due to age or health concerns. Others just thought they could not risk being away from their families for such a long time and others felt it was outside of our core mission, as there were so many families of Angels right here in our own country who needed our support.

No doubt this was an ambitious project. I, too, was not completely sure this was the right thing to do. After visiting the children of Kibeho, however, I knew I had to return, and I hoped that others would be willing to join me.

CHAPTER ELEVEN

Angels Army Africa

We needed to have at least twelve to fifteen skilled playground builders to achieve our goal. The plan was to be in Africa for a full seven days, while allowing three days for travel. There were many members of the "Angels Army" who wanted to go to Africa but could not. Those unable to make the trip supported those who could travel in many ways. Money, clothes, supplies and equipment were all donated by the very generous band of volunteers so that the "Angels Army" could be adequately represented.

My wife, Kathy Lavin, is the quintessential unsung hero. Throughout the successful existence of the Where Angels Play Foundation and the playground projects that so respectfully honored young beautiful lives, Kathy worked tirelessly behind the scenes.

Kathy assisted Executive Director Mary Kate Herbert, our daughter, in her many duties. Accounting, marketing, merchandise sales, and volunteer coordination were all part of her skill set. Kathy's most valuable asset was being the compassionate voice and ear to the Angels' families as they navigated the many emotional experiences associated with the spiritual roller coaster that accompanies every Where Angels Play endeavor.

Kathy had expressed real fear and concern about going to a developing country, replete with its violent history, poverty and disease. The lack of medical and housing infrastructure concerned her greatly. But like always, she put her fears aside, started to get her medications and yellow fever shots and agreed that, although reluctantly, she was all in for this adventure.

Having Kathy on board was a major boost to my confidence that this Africa humanitarian trip would be a success.

The opportunity to travel to Rwanda was extended to the entire Angels Army. I hoped I would get the right combination of people to deliver a talented and physically strong group of volunteers who could withstand the taxing travel requirements, as well as be productive on the construction site. What I got at the end of the day was the perfect combination of brains, brawn, and heart. Following is a break down of the team.

Mud Ducks and Workhorses:

Retired Fire Captains, Brian McGorty, Brian Dolaghan, Herman Peters and Ray Colavito provided our team with construction know-how, brute strength and a work ethic second to none.

Brian McGorty, the ever quick-witted humanitarian, was born for this trip. He had been the heart and conscience of the NJFMBA for years and this trip suited him perfectly. Brian spent his entire life trying to make a difference in the world. I knew the minute this idea was hatched that Brian would have to be a part of this journey.

Brian's effort at the cement mixer and upbeat attitude kept everyone on their toes throughout the trip. The personal interaction with the poorest or richest among us was always with great respect as Brian is a man of the people, all people, and he led by his charitable and generous example. When Brian grew his beard and his hair long he could remind you of Santa Claus. It wasn't long before the children of Rwanda would be referring to Brian as Poppa Noel.

Brian Dolaghan was perhaps one of the most knowledgeable construction people we had with us. Brian could do plumbing and electrical work as well as masonry. He could handle just about any tool and had a knack for problem solving and troubleshooting. All that combined with the physical strength that belied his age. In Brian, we had the perfect individual with whom to build a playground.

Herman Peters is a mountain of a man and has a heart to match. Herman anchored the cement team on every Where Angels Play build.

He is so strong, which is necessary for cement work, but he was even more valuable with his knowledge of concrete. He knew what consistency to mix, how much to order and of course to train others in the art of "mud-duckery." His gruff sense of humor and colorful language were a bonus and he played tough guy most of the time until a young child would smile and thank him for his work or sing to him and then he'd melt and cry like a baby.

Ray Colavito was a surprise traveler as he was new to our projects. Ray is strong as an ox and had worked concrete for years with Herman. Herman vouched for Ray that he would be a great fit for our team. Herman couldn't have been more right about Ray. Ray was dedicated to our cause instantly. He marveled at the poverty of Rwanda and he openly showed compassion and generosity toward the native Rwandan people. Ray could outwork most of us and was involved in every aspect of the trip. From the build, the Catholic Mass and negotiations with the nuns Ray seemed to be everywhere. Ray gave every ounce of his soul to the project, and we all watched his spiritual tank fill up before our eyes.

Ground Crew and "Jack of All Trades"

Kevin "Pops" Kennedy is the quintessential "go-to" for just about any task you need to get done and get done quickly. Pops, we affectionately call him because he was the oldest guy on the hockey team but funny enough he wasn't nearly old enough to be called Pops with our crew of elder statesmen. But we called him Pops nonetheless.

Pops could run a jackhammer, a drill gun or thread a needle, it didn't matter. He worked so hard and did everything with a smile. Pops would give his last nickel to someone in need and he loved watching the kids in Kibeho watching us. Kevin "Pops" Kennedy was a joy to be around and his emotional roller coaster was fun to watch.

Battalion Chief Joe Wurtzbacher was the steady quiet type until he relaxed with a few beers. Joe came on board the African trip with an open mind and an open heart. He was our thoughtful guy and someone to care for others when they needed a break or an aspirin or some water. Joe looked after the older members, especially my brother Butch, when he was to fall ill. On the build site, Joe was the consummate team player and skillful enough to be able to jump in with any team that was struggling or needed some help.

Brian Dolaghan introduced Ray Cerwinski to me and in turn to the Angels Army. Ray is a skilled mechanic in just about every discipline. He had helped me put a heater in my house and we were talking about upcoming trips and he jumped all over it. To have a skilled guy like Ray on the team was a Godsend. Ray was among the biggest and strongest of all of us and he had knowledge of tools most did not. He would often remain quiet during a debate over how to proceed on the job and just watch. Then when someone would say, "Hey Ray, what do you think?" Then of course he stated as a matter of fact that we should try it his way. Of course, his way was always the best or easiest way to remedy the problem. Ray loved the African folks and told me he preferred to go to places outside the country to help people, because he wanted to help the most needy and most impoverished people in the world.

The Engineers

Retired Captain Mike Candelori was the most experienced of my mechanical types. Mike was the one guy I had to have on the trip due to his knowledge of the actual playground apparatus. The nuts and bolts assembly would fall on Mike's experienced hands. With few exceptions, Mike was the guy who knew which playground post should go where, and which panel or slide matched up with what deck.

Mike would prepare in the morning, work all day and in the evening want to talk about how we could adjust things the next day to be even more efficient. Mike played hard and worked even harder. His generous deeds were only surpassed by his generous heart and wallet.

Always the first to donate to any charity, he'd do anything for almost anybody and usually did. His dance with the local Kibeho girls during a traditional African ritual is the stuff of legend. Mike was a quiet traveler while aboard the long flight but, on the continent of Africa he was a force to be reckoned with.

Deputy Chief Craig Hopkins was a no brainer for the trek to Africa. He was always the first to sign up for any place in the United States we would travel. As one of the few still active firefighters in our group, Craig would always find a way to get time off from work. Either sacrificing his personal or vacation time, Craig always put Where Angels Play projects first. He was first to donate and work on our behalf. Craig's loyalty to the Angels Army was second to none. He knew quite a lot about mechanics and how things worked and when he got finished explaining to everyone how to best get it done, he wound up doing it himself anyway. His energy was impressive; he could stay up all night (and often did) and then not miss a beat working so hard the next day. His observation of the Rwandan surroundings were classic, and he enjoyed our adventure as much as we all enjoyed him.

Medical Team

Gino Ambrosio—before we knew Dr. Jim Creighton was going to be a part of our travel team in Rwanda, we knew we had to have a good medical person with us. Gino Ambrosio was our man. A fellow burn camp counselor, Gino was a burn nurse and a no-nonsense health professional. He knew what was healthy for us and what was not. If we got cut, he could stitch us up. If we overheated, he brought IV's with him. He was always ready to supply medicines if need be. From a headache to dehydration, Gino was on the scene to put our fears at ease. Just having him on the trip was a comfort to so many of us, especially because we had no idea what insect or plant was waiting for us around the bend. In addition to Gino's medical background, he worked right alongside the rest of us. For documentation purposes, Gino was the social media guy. He always got the best photo and knew how to dress them up with graphics and an accompanying quote that captured the essence of what we were doing so far away from home. Gino spread the word of the Where Angels Play Foundation to anyone who would listen and expanded our network to the betterment of our mission.

The Business Men:

Tony Wieners, who served as my travel partner on our first trip to Africa, was the former President of the New Jersey State Police Benevolent Association and with 33,000 members that was no easy job. Tony provided the experience of a seasoned traveler and the leadership needed to give direction to us when we sometimes strayed away from our core mission. Tony knew the landscape socially and culturally in Rwanda, and it served him and all of us very well. He knew where to go or not to go, what to eat or not to eat, and what maladies to watch out for and what remedies we would need to counteract them. A real confidante for me for Union issues or political concerns, Tony brought with him a professional presence and a confidence that put us all at ease. He was always positive and had the ability to appreciate the moments we were experiencing. His height of 6'6" brought long stares from the Rwandan people. He was a giant for sure, but a gentle giant with a heart of gold and an intellect that came in handy many times throughout our journey. Tony was a world traveler who had visited some of the poorest places on earth as he worked for Habitat for Humanity. His worldly knowledge suited our group and our mission just right.

Mark Goode, our lone Canadian member, was also a successful businessman from Orillia, Ontario. Mark put together Where Angels Play Canada for us and chaired our first international playground build for Angel, Jacob Noble. Mark had fundraising skills, organizational skills, and social skills that placed him smack in the middle of every business deal we needed to get done in Africa. From navigating the airports and customs or how to work the airlines for seats and accommodations we learned from Mark every step of the way. I would often confer with Mark about how to split up luggage or commandeer a bus. Mark had a way of negotiating food and ice-cold beer exactly at the precise time we needed it. Mark worked the playground build and basketball court, while at the same time communicating to a local businessman of the supplies we would need to make our trip run smoothly and efficiently.

Security and Protection:

Chris McGowan Retired Colonel United States Army—having Chris and Shara McGowan on the trip to Rwanda was an absolute blessing and provided a feeling of safety and security to our entire team. Chris grew up next door to me and I have known him—since he was thirteen years old—for almost 40 years. Having attended the United States Military Academy at West Point and rising through the ranks to Colonel, Chris is the all-American soldier. He served with distinction and heroism in too many conflicts and deployments for me to count. I've been able to stay in touch with him through the years while in places like Afghanistan, Korea, or Germany. The obvious skills of a battle-tested American Army officer, Chris exhibited that and more. His strong faith and his kindly nature are what make him even more impressive in my eyes. Having him with us brought instant security, credibility and passion for helping others as proud Americans. On the playground itself his engineering background would support all the rest of our builders in the most professional way.

If Chris wasn't impressive enough, he was joined by another West Point graduate and Army officer, his wife, Shara McGowan. Shara's talents are as impressive as her husband's and after retiring from the Army, now works as a Special Agent for the FBI out of the Kansas City office. A highly decorated Special Agent, Shara has a deep commitment to the United States and its security as she works in counterterrorism. So if we all felt safer for having this American heroine with us, who could blame us. Shara's brilliance and dedication as Special Agent was only surpassed by her commitment as a wife and mother. Shara brought along a heart as big as all outdoors and she was the perfect partner for my wife, Kathy, to handle all the logistic and practical duties of our mission.

Family Support

With an all-star cast with which I was blessed to travel, perhaps one of the most vital elements of our team, for me personally, was my family. To have three of my brothers and an amazing nephew with me was magical.

Butch, my oldest brother and godfather, provided the wisdom, heart and compassion to an already blessed group of individuals. Butch's religious devotion fit nicely with the folks on the pilgrimage to the Blessed Mother. Butch often acted as our liaison to our fellow U.S. travel partners. Despite being the senior member of the Angel Army, Africa, Butch could amaze his much younger co-workers with his strength and endurance on the Mud Duck team. Impressing Herman with his endurance and grit at the cement mixer, Butch never wanted to break unless the job was completed for the day.

My brother Bob Lavin, retired Battalion Fire Chief from Elizabeth Fire Department, was all of the above for our team. Bob could provide spiritual guidance and support through his practice of Qi-Gong. He could entertain with an impromptu dance or converse with one of the native Rwandans who spoke no English and still get his point across. A proud Vietnam Veteran and a hero of mine since I was a small boy, Bob brought insight and perspective and a work ethic everyone seemed to respect and follow. For me, he was my counselor, soundboard and a leader who could take over the build or meeting whenever I needed.

Pat Lavin, my business partner for years and retired police officer, rounded out the Lavin brothers' team. Pat brought law and order with him and a sense of fairness and diplomacy. From a lifetime of working two, sometimes three jobs at the same time, Pat knew the art of multi-tasking. When chaos seemed to reign, Pat was the calm one to maintain peace and calm, despite being distracted at times with matters of concern back home and missing his family. Pat would work anyone under the table. No injury ever stopped Pat from completing a job. As the heat and humidity were bearing down on us all, Pat seemed to be almost immune to it. Resting only when necessary, Pat was indeed one of the workhorse Americans that made the entire group proud. Pat watched over his older brothers and made sure they had everything they needed.

Nephew Dan Beirne—as the youngest member of our team, Danny brought unbridled enthusiasm and boundless energy. One of the brightest members of the entire Lavin clan, Danny had climbed the ranks of the local union to eventually become the President of NJFMBA Local #9. It was Danny, more than any of our crew, who marveled and appreciated the wonder of the Rwandan people. He worked with the local men as if he were part of their tribe. To watch Danny's energy and magnificent attitude on the work site was infectious to the rest of the team. Danny had left his ailing Dad at home and was working extra hard in honor of Dan, Sr. In a way, Danny made us feel that his Dad was being represented and was right there with the rest of us.

So there you have the team, 20 spirited, generous, courageous folks that would sacrifice their health, finances, and their time with family, to try to bring joy to the poorest and most needy on the face of the earth.

The time spent there would create an experience and a bond that would never be broken.

Shara and Kathy deliver breakfast Rwandan style

Joe Wurtzbacher joins Team Lavin at Kigali International Airport

CHAPTER TWELVE

Worlds Collide

From JFK airport in New York, on KLM Airlines, the twenty members of the African Angels Army representing the Where Angels Play Foundation began their adventure together. We experienced a stop over in Amsterdam for a quick layover then on to Kigali, Rwanda. Just before the trip, Brian McGorty had told me of a possible contact he had made with a medical doctor, who was originally from Jersey City, New Jersey, and had lived in Africa for the last eighteen years. Brian's cousin, Ann, had reconnected with her classmate, Beth Creighton, who was the sister of Dr. Jim Creighton. Brian told me that Dr. Jim had just retired from medicine and was filming documentaries while living with his family in Kigali, Rwanda and wanted to know if we would be interested in allowing them to document our entire trip from start to finish.

I think I rolled my eyes at Brian because, how could that possibly be true, that our luck would be that good. You see many of our team had concerns for our health and fear about somehow getting some disease in this foreign land and now a medical doctor was willing to travel with us? On top of that, his team would film and document our trip at no cost?

"C'mon Brian," I said, "there's no way our luck is that good. What are the odds, and he's from Jersey?"

Brian responded, "Not only that Bill, his wife is the director of the CDC for all of Rwanda!" I only half believed Brian, even though he'd never let me down before. But I thought to myself this was really too good to be true!

We took this long flight with nervous anticipation, gathering at the bulkhead area to talk with one another, anxious about what kind of a world awaited us. We had heard many stories of Africa, Yellow Fever, Malaria, and, of course, the horror stories associated with the genocide. Would it be safe? How would the people treat us? Would we be welcomed? We had also heard of the beauty of Africa, the landscape, the waterfalls, and the animals. We couldn't imagine what this strange new world had in store for us.

The flight was long for sure but when we touched down in Kigali we felt not only a sigh of relief but also energy, an excitement to explore and deliver on our promise of a playground. I had arranged the shipment of the playground along with our tools on a container ship that I was notified had arrived in Kibeho a good two weeks before our arrival. In addition to the playground we also shipped twenty-six bicycles thanks to Rebecca and Steve Kowalski, the parents of Sandy Hook Elementary School Angel seven-year old Chase Kowalski.

Rebecca and Steve had become great friends of ours after Chase's playground was constructed in Normandy Beach, New Jersey. The Kowalski family is emblematic of the incredibly strong families we were blessed to call family as we worked with them through the Where Angels Play Foundation building process. In honor of Chase, they had created the Race for Chase Foundation that taught young children to run, bike and swim and complete a triathlon just as Chase had so remarkably done as a seven-year old. When I came back from Rwanda the first time and told Rebecca of the poverty there and that a bicycle was like owning a car, Rebecca suggested that I take bicycles with us to distribute to change the lives of families even more. David Fowler from Bikes for Kids, a great foundation who would re-purpose bicycles for underprivileged children, donated twenty-six bicycles representing Chase and all the 26 Angels from Sandy Hook, to be gifted to Rwandan men and women we encountered.

With the playground, our tools, equipment, and bicycles awaiting our arrival we walked off the KLM jet through Customs and boarded a bus for our hotel in Kigali.

When we arrived at our residence in Kigali, it was after midnight Rwanda time. We were exhausted, hungry and thirsty. Our Rwandan liaison had let us down and had no food or drink or any type of reception to welcome our 20 weary travelers from America.

However, we met for the first time at the entrance to the Kigali Residence hotel, Dr. Jim Creighton and his beautiful wife Gene. These two actually did exist!!! In what would become a recurring theme, Dr. Jim and Gene came to our rescue, with a cooler full of ice-cold Mutzig beer and bouquets of flowers for my wife Kathy and Shara McGowan the two females on our team. Gene and Jim graciously welcomed us all to Rwanda and a lifelong friendship with the Creighton family had instantly begun.

The welcome we received from the Creightons more than made up for the lack of attention to detail from our African travel connection. With advice and logistical information, Dr. Jim and Gene were lifesavers and we immediately felt safe and confident that we could navigate this beautiful, remarkable country.

Dr. Jim began filming and interviewing our team almost immediately. Pat Lavin happened to strike up a conversation with one of the members of Dr. Jim's film crew, a tall thin Rwandan native named Yannick. Pat bummed a cigarette from Yannick. This pleasant young man and Pat talked for quite some time. Pat was surprised to know Yannick spoke English. Yannick seemed eager to speak with all of us and seemed genuinely fascinated with the collection of white Americans that had just arrived in his country.

Pat introduced me to Yannick. Yannick had a very distinctive cut across his left cheek, and his left ear appeared to have been cut in two. It looked as if his injury must have been very painful, and I noticed he would constantly squint his eyes as if the lights were hurting him.

Dr. Jim had some other members of his film crew with him that night. Maurice was also tall and thin and very talkative. Robert was the lead cameraman and seemed to just smile. At first he said very little. Yannick stood out to my brother and me because of his welcoming personality and his obvious scar. We couldn't help but think he must have been injured during some sort of battle during the genocide.

The subject turned to how hungry our guys were and so we inquired with some of the locals at the hotel. Dr. Jim said he thought there was a pizza place not far from where we were staying and he decided to send Yannick to pick up 12 pizzas. As surprised as we were that they had pizza in Africa, we were so hungry we really would have eaten just about anything.

Yannick eagerly volunteered to go for the pizza and away he went while the rest of our crew drank Mutzig beer and got to know Jim, Gene and their 14-year-old son, Sean as well as Maurice and Robert. The entire gang got along so well and Sean, the doctor's son, enjoyed educating us all about Rwanda, a country he appeared to love, and the history of the genocide.

Dr. Jim explained that Yannick had been cut with a machete when he was about 3 ½ years old and that his family in its entirety was murdered in the genocide. In fact, all of his employees had suffered the loss of their family members as a result of the genocide. We were horrified at that thought and to think this happened only about 23 years earlier. It was sobering and scary at the same time. Our hearts were breaking at hearing their stories and meeting people who were victims of the genocide first hand. It was almost too much for us to comprehend, such violence and then my thoughts turned to Yannick.

It was difficult to imagine how anyone could hit a child in the face with a machete. The Creighton's explained that actually Yannick was one of the lucky ones who survived and that almost a million Rwandans were murdered in the genocide including thousands and thousands of children and infants. It was overwhelmingly sad and yet Maurice and Robert were here with us, smiling and talking with us as if nothing had ever happened. We would later learn that both Maurice and Robert had lost their parents as well.

The topic of conversation finally moved on to our playground mission... where we would be staying, how we should travel, and where to get supplies. I was thrilled to know that Dr. Jim, Gene and Sean and their crew would be traveling and staying with us the entire visit. They would prove invaluable to us.

Yannick finally came back with the pizza. Different than we were accustomed to, the pizza was very tasty none-the-less. Our crew devoured the pizza pies in minutes and couldn't thank Yannick enough for making the midnight run. We noticed some blood and scratches on his elbow and asked what happened. Yannick explained that a taxi here in Kigali was actually a moped and as he was coming back from the store sitting on the back of this moped, holding 12 pizza pies, the moped was struck by an automobile, and he and the driver were knocked onto the street.

Yannick assured us proudly that he had not dropped the pizza despite being knocked to the ground and almost run over by the car. He excused himself and said he now had to go to the hospital to get treatment for his injuries. As he limped away we all looked at one another and our jaws dropped. This young guy with the scar across his face delivered our pizzas after being hit by a car on a moped? We all thought how remarkably dedicated to his job and to us he had been, but we also thought how absolutely crazy a story and hoped he wasn't hurt too badly. We all felt terrible that our hunger was the cause of his accident. Dr. Jim and Gene accompanied Yannick to the emergency room in King Faisal Hospital where he underwent X-rays and an MRI well into the early morning. To everyone's great relief Yannick's injuries were soft tissue and would heal with time.

The next day Yannick explained that the accident was his fault, because he had told the driver to hurry up because there were "umucyire's" (rich guys in Kinyarwanda), waiting to eat and they were very hungry. I was dumb-founded to hear him say that and assured him it was not his fault and how grateful we all were to him for such an act of selflessness. He just shrugged as if it were no big deal. This guy Yannick was impressive in so many ways, every member of our team agreed. Just how impressive he was, we had only begun to appreciate.

Kibeho kids patiently wait the completion of their new park

CHAPTER THIRTEEN

The Land of a Thousand Hills

Our trip would begin the next morning as our bus toured the capital city of Kigali. Its signature round convention hall all lit up looked like a giant carousel. Between that structure, many modern buildings, and landscaped parks we thought this was just like any other major city in the world and construction seemed everywhere!

Busy streets with modern cars, countless mopeds and motorcycles filled the bustling streets in and around the city. Young Sean Creighton got on the bus microphone and, acted as our tour guide, pointing out President Kagame's residence complete with armed soldiers and AK 47 automatic rifles. In fact, the armed soldiers seemed to be at every major intersection and modern facility. The government buildings seemed especially guarded. This was unsettling to us but Sean assured us it was commonplace here in Rwanda, and there was nothing for us to fear.

A few of our members, Gino and Craig, tried to take pictures of the soldiers but with a stern wag of the finger the soldiers communicated that would not be tolerated. We continued to tour the beautiful bustling city of Kigali with eyes wide open, but with some caution we accompanied Dr. Jim and the film crew as well as the American tourist group who were on a pilgrimage to Kibeho to honor the feast day of "Our Lady of Kibeho."

This week was the anniversary of the Blessed Mother's appearance to three teenage girls at the Mother of the Word School. In 1981 it was reported and widely believed that the Virgin Mary foretold the genocide that would happen almost 13 years later. We were excited to learn that the site of the apparitions was actually the school that was chosen by Rwandan clergy to build our playground. Later that day, the pilgrims and our African Angels Army were given a tour of the Rwandan Genocide Museum. Basically built on the mass grave of genocide victims, this beautiful marble structure housed videos, artifacts, weapons, and testimonials documenting the horrific and sad history of the 100 days in 1994 that senselessly cost the lives of almost one million Rwandans.

All of our members were profoundly affected and left with a sadness that was palpable. "How could something like this happen, and so recently?" asked Tony Wieners.

Before we got back in the bus, Dr. Jim and part of his film crew, (Sean, Maurice, Dixon and Robert) set up their cameras and equipment to interview a few of us to get our reaction. While we were waiting for Sean to return from the bus with a new battery for the camera, I spoke with Maurice, Dixon and Robert about what we had just seen inside the museum. I noticed none of them had joined us on the tour of the museum and asked why.

Maurice explained, "It is too difficult to enter this sacred place. Most likely our parents and other family members are buried here."

He pointed to the marble area below and all around us.

Robert further explained, "This was really a mass grave where bodies were taken because there were so many who could not be identified and were collected in this one gigantic burial site."

I was speechless and felt so terrible for these young men. They were working on a documentary for us while struggling with their own reality of grief and loss.

When the video began for me to respond to what I'd witnessed I could only speak of the tremendous respect I had for the crew and was astonished at their courage and grace—how they held it together as they told their story—I couldn't even begin to imagine.

It was upon walking back to the bus that Maurice told me that Yannick had spent the last night in the hospital but was treated for his bruises and scrapes and then released. He had no broken bones or serious injuries and was taking the day off. I expressed how impressed I was with Yannick to the film crew and they agreed. He was a special individual who always put his duties and responsibilities before all else. Obviously, he proved this fact the night before with his incredible pizza delivery at all costs.

Back aboard the bus, we silently sat in our private thoughts. Some of us prayed, others wiped tears from their eyes, and others simply stared out at the Rwandan countryside which grew ever more beautiful with each passing mile.

That night we attended a fundraiser for the Rwandan Autism Foundation. It was hosted at the beautiful Marriott Hotel in downtown Kigali. We were all treated like royalty. The food was American style and quite good. I was invited to speak to the guests about the Where Angels Play Foundation. Through an interpreter, I thanked them for their work on behalf of the Autism community.

We knew we had an early morning bus ride to Kibeho the following day so our team ate and promptly excused themselves and headed back to the residence where we were staying. We would finally begin the work we had traveled so far to do.

At 5:00 a.m. the sun was already up and a small jitney bus arrived for our journey through the countryside. This was not the bus we had expected but it was the only game in town. I met Jean Paul, our guide, for the very first time. Jean Paul was hired and assigned to us through a third party travel partner.

He was a handy man contractor who would assist us with our build and help us acquire any and all materials or local workforce we would need. Jean Paul was an extremely pleasant fellow, he was strong and capable and apologized for the bus. He explained that he had been given the wrong information about the numbers requiring bus transportation. Jean Paul, a 40-something Rwandan, was a humble man with a wife and children. Jean Paul was hard working and had a knack for being able to find anything or anyone we needed to complete our playground construction project. He would prove invaluable and a loyal friend.

Because the bus was half the size we needed, we had to leave five of our team behind, as well as the luggage. My wife, Kathy, brother Butch, Shara and Chris McGowan and Mark Goode all agreed to hang back and take a second bus with the luggage and the pilgrims. They would take the five-hour ride to Kibeho saying dozens of prayers and the rosary dedicated to the Blessed Mother. They got their collective fill of religion from the devout Catholic pilgrims.

Meanwhile, the remaining 15 Americans packed themselves into the tiny commuter bus with some personal tools and belongings and set off to the small village of Kibeho. As we climbed deeper into the countryside, the green lush trees became more and more beautiful, the mountains more majestic, the waterfalls more spectacular, and the people more and more scarce. We all had expected a much more dry and brown landscape and were surprised at the emerald green hills and mountains.

The roadway turned from blacktop to gravel to dirt and upon arriving in Butare, the halfway point, the road just disappeared completely into a rocky pathway that barely made room for the tired old commuter bus that chugged and rambled ever closer to our destination.

In Butare, we found a small outside bar where we stretched our legs and found some iced-cold Mutzig beer and took our first bathroom break. The second stop would be just a bathroom on the side of the road.

We felt we were slowly disappearing from civilization and into a whole new wondrous world of nature, animals, and the smiling native people of Rwanda's beautiful countryside.

When we pulled over to take pictures of the fields of tea and the lush green mountains that stretched for miles the landscape started to come alive with people. Farmers of all shapes and sizes, young and old began to pop their heads up out of the fields to try and get a peek at the bus full of white men. They stared as if they had never seen another white man before, and for some they truly had not. We were told we were a rare sight in these parts.

Without exception every man, woman and child waved to us with, at first, curiosity and then a great big smile. Every person we encountered seemed so happy to see us. Perhaps they instinctively knew that we were there to help them. We had brought with us many gifts and candy to treat the children as well as T-shirts that our Angel families had so happily donated to share with our new African friends. With each gift or piece of candy we always drew a crowd of more and more people. No matter how much we distributed, food, candy or clothing it was swallowed up instantly and we soon realized it would never be close to being enough for these people who were in need of so much.

It took over five hours to reach the religious retreat compound where we would all be staying. It was clean and well maintained with plumbing that worked just fine. It was part of a Catholic parish that housed several priests and some church administrators. All the pilgrims would be staying at the hotel/rectory along with us. We were two to a room with simple beds, a toilet and hot water for a shower. It wasn't the Hilton but compared to what we imagined it was more than comfortable. Soon guilt would begin to set in with most of us, as we quickly realized that less than 100 feet away, the people who lived in Kibeho had no electricity, no running water, no indoor plumbing, and lived in shacks with dirt floors.

Compared to the native Rwandans of Kibeho, we were living in paradise. Quickly we began to appreciate all the things we, as Americans, take for granted every single day. Electricity, plumbing, food, air conditioning, paved roads, cars, and bicycles... these folks had none of any of that.

We learned that only one percent of the population enjoyed electricity in the entire nation. We soon felt spoiled and noticed while these people had so little they seemed quite content and happy.

Kathy, Chris, Shara, Butch, Mark and all the pilgrims soon arrived shortly after us. They transported the luggage and the rest of our tools as well. That night we ate a big native Rwandan meal of rice, chicken, vegetables and Coca-Cola. It was surprisingly quite tasty. Mark Goode remarkably somehow scored some more ice-cold Mutzig beer, and our crew celebrated our safe arrival to Kibeho in style.

Herman, our oversized teddy bear, entertained us with stories. Chris and Shara reported on the holy and prayerful journey they shared with the pilgrims, and as firefighters are inclined to do, we drank beer and told stories as it got dark until we realized we had quite a lot of work to do in the early morning and needed to call it a night.

As the night drew to a close and we all started heading to our respective rooms, Yannick showed up with a couple of fresh bandages, but with his big toothy smile bigger than ever. The gang welcomed him back with a hero's salute, and he grabbed a cold beer and settled into some late night conversation. Eventually my brother Bob and I were left to interview Yannick. This new fascinating friend who we became to like so well was eager to tell his story. I'm not sure if it was Bob's idea or mine but the things Yannick told us were so amazing, we decided to video him on our iPhone. We were, sort of, turning the table on Dr. Jim's film crew a bit.

Yannick began to tell Bob and I about his personal story. The scar on his face he confirmed was from the attack from a neighbor who had slashed his face and ear with a machete. He also told us that his mother, father, brothers, sisters, and grandparents were all killed in the Genocide of 1994.

Listening to him was heartbreaking but he was quite proud of the fact that he survived. The next thing that Yannick said was and is still is the most incredible and startling thing that for me defines this young man and child of God. Yannick explained to Bob and I that he has forgiven the man named, Kayibanda who had attacked him. Furthermore, Yannick has forgiven all the soldiers who had murdered his family and the families of Rwandans everywhere. In fact, he then said, he visits Kayibanda in prison and sometimes brings him money so he can have extra to eat in prison.

Stunned silence—Brother Bob and I looked at each other with incredulous stares. Yannick repeated, "Yes its true, and it was something I had to do not to save Kayibanda but, in fact, it was a gift to myself, like putting down a great burden."

If he hadn't forgiven he would forever be limited in what he could achieve and he would never be free, he told us. *Wow!* We both finally mouthed silently to one another. How could this be possible for some-one to forgive such brutality and violence? It would take time for us to learn and appreciate the power of forgiveness and the freedom it bestows.

This lesson of forgiveness is perhaps Yannick's greatest gift and most important blessing we received upon traveling to this bewildering, fascinating and blessed country.

Dr. Jim Creighton interviews Bill outside of the Genocide Museum

CHAPTER FOURTEEN

Breaking Ground

The Build at Mother of the Word School

On November 27, 2017, at 5 a.m. all 20 members of Where Angels Play traveled a quick one-mile bus ride to the Mere du Verbe School on a hillside in the tiny village of Kibeho. The Mere du Verbe School translates in English to "Mother of the Word." This is the name the Blessed Mother referred to herself according to the visionaries who were visited by the Virgin Mary in 1981. These apparitions happened in and around the school and predicted the genocide. Therefore, the name was changed to Mere du Verbe or "Mother of the Word."

Mother of the Word School was managed by Principal Sister Bridget while Sister Emilene acted as our liaison to the school.

The Mother of the Word School is a concrete structure and the courtyard is covered almost entirely with red brick pavers which were plentiful in Rwanda. We soon realized the site chosen within the walled schoolyard was not ideal for two reasons.

First, the ground was hard and covered in brick and would not be a good soft surface for children to play. Second, it was inside a walled school and the children of the village would not have access to it.

We immediately asked the physical fitness teacher if there was an alternative site to position the playground. He suggested a beautiful bluff that had a sandy surface and overlooked a beautiful meadow of trees and flowers growing out of the tall grass. While this new site was aesthetically beautiful, the real beauty of it lay in the fact that not only would the students from Mother of the Word School have access to the playground, all the children from the village and beyond would be able to utilize the park.

We began to unpack the posts, tools and slides for the playground from a storage barn the school used for discarded desks and other equipment. We needed to do an inventory of all the matching playground pieces. Kids Around the World, our great partners in this charitable event, had actually shipped two playgrounds. One playground was for us to build right there at the school, and another smaller unit to be picked up and installed by volunteer members of another charity some months later. It was a critical operation to be sure we had all the parts for our particular structure and, of course, match up properly with the numbered posts and the directions we had been provided.

Julie and Bruce Rearick, our representatives from Kids Around the World, were magnificent partners. They had trained us, helped us color code our equipment, and provided counsel on how to navigate the procurement of building supplies needed in a foreign land. Julie and Bruce had done dozens of playgrounds around the world, with as many as 40 in the island nation of Haiti alone. True humanitarians, the Rearicks' encouragement gave me the confidence I needed to believe we could complete our ambitious mission.

We all created an assembly line to carry out the parts and align them in an orderly fashion. We began to notice the heat we were working in. Sweating profusely, most of us were in our late 50's and early 60's but in relatively good physical condition, but noticed we were becoming short of breath. Kibeho, Rwanda is more than 6,000 feet above sea level and the air was quite thin and certainly not anything with which we were familiar.

My brother Charles, "Butch" we all call him, was the oldest member of our team and probably stronger than most, but had not been eating and drinking enough since he arrived in Africa for fear of getting a stomach virus. Between his lack of fluids, food, the heat and the altitude... Butch became lightheaded and fainted. This was quite scary for us all as we had no clue he hadn't been eating, and feared it was a far more serious illness. Because we had Dr. Jim with us as well as Gino, a registered nurse, Butch was treated with immediate care and was taken via Dr. Jim's car to the nearby hospital in Butare. Butch responded quickly to fluids and oxygen and fortunately bounced back quickly and only stayed in the hospital for a very brief time.

Butch's incident actually turned out to be a warning for the rest of us and we were more mindful of the heat and altitude. We encouraged each other to drink plenty of water to eat right and to take frequent breaks. We focused on keeping an eye on the team. We began a rotation, relieving one another on the more strenuous tasks.

On this day we organized our equipment, did inventory for our hardware, cleaned the job site, and marked out the location for our posts to be ready for the next day's build.

When we completed our tasks for the day, we were feeling good about our chances of completing the playground on time. We were then told that tomorrow, the 28th of November, was, in fact, the feast of "Our Lady of Kibeho."

Thousands upon thousands of Africans from all over the continent would be making a pilgrimage to Kibeho for a huge outdoor Catholic Mass. This meant that working on the playground would be greatly frowned upon, and we were advised to take the day off. We all decided to attend the Mass and were amazed at the throngs of people surrounding the outside altar on a mountaintop. As far as you could see, African men, women and children crowded together to get a view of the statue of the Virgin Mary and listen to the Mass that was celebrated by almost 50 priests and bishops.

It was hot and sunny and the Mass lasted over four hours. Many of our crew are not very religious, spiritual yes, but churchgoers—not so much. So while it was a beautiful spectacle to see, four hours pressed the patience of many of us, including myself. I marveled once again at the offertory procession and the collection of the poorest of the poor offering to the church anything they could. I felt sad and awkward about this, but I learned they are very proud people.

Ray Colavito, a rough and tumble firefighter from West New York, New Jersey, sat next to me. Ray joked about the basket coming before us.

He (not so softly) jokingly whispered, "They're banging us again!"

Everyone in ear-shot cracked up laughing, and it reminded us that we were a different sort of spiritual gang from Jersey.

Colorful, beautiful, impressive, sacredly holy and tearfully sad and ironic—all at the same time—the experience of the Mass, we all agreed, would be unforgettable.

Later that day, we got together to plan our construction and realized we now were under the gun to finish as we had lost an entire day due to the feast and Mass. In addition, it was discovered that many of our hand tools, levels and wrenches were missing. They must have been stolen at the port upon inspection into the harbor city of Mombasa, Kenya.

We would be further challenged to have a smooth build.

I met with Jean Paul that evening and we decided we could hire some local men to assist us on the build to overcome some of our challenges. Jean Paul was confident we could hire as many men as we needed. He asked that we not pay them until completion of the project so as not to attract too many others in the area who would be eager to work for U.S. currency—another stark reminder of the abject poverty that surrounded us.

Eventually Dr. Jim, Maurice, Sean, Robert, Dixon and Yannick visited with us to get some footage and comments from our team. A new member of their team arrived as well, Charles Wakamumba, a tall good-looking fellow that fit in well with the rest of the gang. Charles and Yannick stayed up with us later than the others, and we engaged in long conversation well into the night.

Yannick became especially emotional with my wife, Kathy, and I that night, describing how his scar branded him as an obvious victim of the genocide. He told us that everywhere he went, his face was a constant reminder to every Rwandan of the horrors and inhumanity of a period of time in their history. Many Rwandans were quite ashamed of their recent past.

Yannick always felt discriminated against and wished and dreamt for a miracle that could somehow repair his face and allow him to live a more normal and inclusive life.

Yannick finally bluntly asked, "Bill, would you know of any plastic surgeons in America who could help to heal my face?" He continued, "I have asked so many people from France, Poland, Germany and the United States who had always promised me they would make it happen but they always left to never be heard from again!"

Both Kathy and I were in tears hearing Yannick pour his heart out about his hardships and pain. I didn't want to promise something when I was unsure I could help him.

I replied, "Yannick, I am a firefighter and do not socialize with doctors as a rule and in fact I do not know any plastic surgeons."

I did say that I would try to make some contacts but in my heart I thought this to be an impossible request to grant. I looked at Kathy, she looked at me and without speaking her eyes expressed... *how in God's name, can we help this poor unfortunate soul?*

We drank a beer or two more and Yannick gravitated to Pops Kennedy and Ray Cerwinski for a night-cap, and then we all returned to bed to be prepared for another 5 a.m. bus ride.

Playground inventory

Surveying the land

CHAPTER FIFTEEN

Men of Steel

The next day Jean Paul was waiting at the build site with 11 additional young men who were thin but made of muscle. They were eager to meet us and get to work. We needed to get the playground equipment from the school that was a good one-quarter mile from the new build site. We loaded up a pick-up truck we had commandeered from the school officials. It was driven down to the edge of the bluff that would be the new home of the playground, still at least 300 yards from where we needed the posts and equipment.

Our team started to unload the pick-up truck with our new Rwandan team of workers. I was at the school at the top of the hill, when my nephew Danny Beirne came running up the hill and excitedly greeted me with a huge grin on his face.

Danny laughed with astonishment, "Uncle Bill, you've gotta come quick and see these guys work; they're literally running as fast as they can with the equipment on their shoulders!"

He insisted I had to see for myself. As I walked to the edge of the elevated road, sure enough I could see these men sprinting as fast as they could unloading the truck in seconds. They soon realized that the truck was too slow and started coming to the school at the top of the hill and began carrying the equipment straight from there to the playground.

These posts and slides were not light and in some cases they weighed over 100 lbs., but they ran with them as if they weighed almost nothing at all. Our team could only smile and laugh and marvel at the sight. These Rwandan workers wanted to impress us, happy and eager to work and be a part of something special. They seemed in competition with one another to move more pieces of equipment faster than the next guy. I'd never seen anything like it before or since in my entire life. I knew at that moment we had all the help we needed to build this playground.

Mike Candelori, Herman Peters, Brian Dolaghan and Brian McGorty were positioning the posts and marking them to be dug the required 32 inches. As we dug with straight bars and shovels, we removed the soft clay and sandy soil dirt as fast as we could.

I'd put up my Angels Army team up against any team in America, but we soon witnessed some work with which we were not familiar. The 11 Kibeho young men, along with Jean Paul, who made 12, we now affectionately called the "apostles," grabbed the shovels and digging bars and like machines began to dig these holes 32 inches deep in a matter of seconds. I'm not exaggerating—rock, sand, mud and dust flew out of these holes as if in fast forward video.

Hole after hole they grabbed the shovels out of our hands and pleaded to be allowed to show how hard and fast they could work. In less than three hours, we had all of our 32 holes dug for our posts. The playground was ready to be built!

Chris McGowan, Mike Candelori, Ray Cerwinski and Craig Hopkins all took turns with the plans—matching up posts to decks to slides to panels. We were missing some posts and that slowed us some, but we figured out how to make do with the equipment we had. Brian McGorty, Butch, Pat and Bob Lavin mixed cement under the watchful supervision of Herman Peters. Pops Kennedy seemed to gravitate to our native helpers and he and Joe Wurtzbacher and Ray Colavito began to become part of the Rwandan band of brothers.

Tony Wieners and Mark Goode worked together on the basketball backboards and posts. Gino filmed it all and pitched in along with Butch wherever needed. Danny Beirne, the youngest of our crew, kept everyone moving and proving to us all that we Americans were just as capable, and, given our age, were doing just fine. So much work was completed on the 29th of November that we breathed a great big sigh of relief that this project was well on its way.

The film crew continued to document the entire operation. We marveled at the pace the "apostles" were working. They worked in mud and rock and most were in bare feet. We decided that the next day any spare pair of shoes or sneakers that we had in our suitcases would be gifted to these wondrous workers.

Shara McGowan and Kathy had to "shake down" the clergy and kitchen staff back at our hotel compound for hardboiled eggs and rolls, and made the best egg sandwiches we ever tasted. It was a great late breakfast and hit the spot. All in all, it turned out to be a perfect day, and we were more than halfway complete.

After a couple more hours of work, we focused on keeping everything we built somewhat level before cementing the posts in place. As we prepared to wrap things up for the day, Pops Kennedy pulled me to the side before he boarded the bus.

He said, "I remember thinking how much I love working with the 'Angels Army' and told you I'd follow you to the ends of the earth, but I never thought you would actually take me there!"

Tony, Mark, Gino and Joe were giving out some T-shirts and gifts to the kids gathered around our bus. When they ran out of the day's supplies, we all boarded the bus and headed back to the hotel, exhausted, sunburned, thirsty, hungry, achy and sore but somehow we never felt better in our lives.

Butch was back with the team sharing a room with brother Pat. Bob and Danny were looking out for him extra closely, but his color was good and his spirits seemed high.

Before we departed from New Jersey, Brian Dolaghan had repeatedly asked me if it was okay to bring cans of Dinty Moore Stew and soup. I was so busy with details, I remember saying "Come on Brian, we'll have food there. What kind of question is that?" And I remember making fun of him about his wanting to bring cans of food.

Well, I soon had to eat my words, as Brian was able to give Butch a can of Dinty Moore Chicken Noodle Soup upon returning from the hospital. Butch devoured the soup because he was so hungry. Pat compared the scene of Butch to Steve McQueen in the movie *Papillon* as he savored every spoonful.

This team of twenty was now a family—taking care of each other, working together, praying for one another, drinking beer together, giving interviews together and sacrificing health and heart, sweat and blood for our new favorite African villagers. Bedtime came early that night.

Brian McGorty, whom the children called
"Papa Noel" and Yannick

The "Apostles" proudly wear the uniforms of our Angels

The strength of a nation

CHAPTER SIXTEEN

The Joy of Giving

November 30th would prove to be a special day in so many ways, and I somehow knew it when I woke from a dream at 3:00 a.m. in our tiny room at the Kibeho hotel compound. I dreamt that the 20 volunteers we had brought were not an arbitrary number. Our 20 travelers represented the 20 children from Sandy Hook and those Angels were really the energy behind each and every one of us. I also dreamt that the 11 Kibeho "apostles" represented each one of the Lavin brothers and sisters and these numbers were meant to bring spiritual meaning to me. I woke up feeling that right there in the middle of Africa was where I was supposed to be at that very moment and everything that I had lived through brought me here for this very purpose.

I cried happy tears for some time. I was wide-awake now feeling quite joyful and decided to walk outside. The sky was lit up with more stars than I could ever count. This was a sight I had only read about in books or seen on National Geographic. Streaks of light flew before my eyes. I saw a shooting star, then a few minutes later another even brighter flash. This was so spectacular a sight, I ran back into our room to wake Kathy. She was having none of it as she moaned loudly, "C'mon are you kidding me right now, I'm sleeping here, I'm exhausted!"

I wouldn't take no for an answer and continued to shake her out of her single bed until she said, "Alright, alright, this is ridiculous now, I'm exhausted."

I laughed as I led her out onto the meadow behind our room. As she looked up at the sky she immediately knew I wasn't kidding—this was worth me waking her up.

At least three more shooting stars would light up the sky like fireworks until we headed back to our room. Kathy was as astonished as I was and thanked me, admitting it was worth waking up for no matter how soundly she had been sleeping. We agreed that we were living a dream moment in our lives and felt blessed to be right where we were at that very moment in time.

The 5:00 a.m. bus ride seemed to be even earlier that day. Everyone was up and eager to get started. Today we knew we had a shot at putting everything together. The rest of the playground was pieced together, with Chris McGowan using his engineering skills to make some key adjustments along with Mike Candelori. Chris would direct the completion of the playground structure. We were now ready for concrete and stabilizing and leveling the unit in place.

So bring on the "mud ducks!" This was the affectionate name we always use for the concrete cement team.

As if we were not impressed enough with the "apostles'" work ethic, we needed to bring the 80 lb. cement bags from the street to the mixing site, a good length of a football field distance of about 100 yards. After our team pushed a couple of wheelbarrows full of mortar mix bags weighing 80 lbs. each, the "apostles" witnessed us huffing and puffing after each trip. As if on cue, our Africans co-workers ran to the top of the hill and each grabbed a bag of mix and placed it on their heads. They ran down the hill balancing the 80 lb. bag on the top of their heads with ease. One after another like giant ants they ran up and down the hill. After dropping the bag on the pile, they ran up a steep incline and began the routine all over again. We all watched in utter amazement, shrugged our shoulders and filmed these physical specimens in awe. In a matter of an hour, we had all the cement necessary to mix and secure our playground.

Tony Wieners and Mark Goode had been working as a team connecting the basketball posts, backboards and rims. Maybe because they were the tallest members of our group, they gravitated towards the new basketball court installation.

Originally we had planned to build the basketball court next to the playground but in an effort to appease Sister Bridget, we decided to remove the school's old rusty basketball court and replace it with a new state-of-the-art glass backboard court. The only problem now was the old basketball posts were buried in four feet of concrete and we had no jackhammer or machine to break it up. Our expert masons thought it was impossible to dig out the posts with shovels, picks or hand tools. But the nuns were insistent on replacing the court so we had to figure out a way.

Brian Dolaghan and Herman Peters thought it was unfair to ask the "apostles" if they could break up the concrete and it would take all day to do so. But once again, we underestimated these amazing men. Jean Paul explained what needed to be done, handed out four metal digging bars and in thirty minutes, both posts were dug faster than if we had a jackhammer.

The men sang in cadence as they dug, smiling, singing, and sweating in unison. We all marveled and imagined what a work force they could be if they had the tools we are blessed with in the United States.

Mark, Tony, Joe, and Pops set up the new basketball rims in an orderly fashion and we all chipped in raising the backboards and set them in cement exactly 10 feet from rim to ground.

Jean Paul remarked to me, "This basketball court is better than the Rwandan National team's practice facility." We were so pleased with our work and glad to make the Marian Nuns happy.

Next we all gathered in a classroom of the Mother of the Word School and asked Jean Paul to bring in the "apostles." One of the single most joyful moments of our trip was about to take place.

Because of the Kowalskis' inspiration and Chase Kowalski's legacy, we had included 26 beautiful bicycles along with the playground container. Provided by Dave Fowler and Bikes for Kids, these 10-speed bicycles were new or like new and in tip-top condition. They also included spare tires, tubes, and repair kits along with baskets to provide storage and transport capability of all types of goods. To appreciate the gift of a bicycle in Rwanda, you have to imagine that to own a car was unheard of and to own a bicycle you were a wealthy individual. Jean Paul equated owning a bike in Rwanda as the equivalent to owning a pickup truck in the United States.

We wanted to reward our local workforce, the "apostles" with a bicycle each and a good weekly salary for all their hard work. We first paid them the equivalent of six months salary each. They cheered and hugged us all. We joked with them, that they needed to work a little harder and arrive a little earlier, except I think our sarcastic humor was lost on them.

I told them, "Guys because we need you to get to work on time, we wanted you to each have your own bicycle."

As Jean Paul repeated my speech in Kinyarwanda, their native tongue, Brian McGorty, Joe, Pops, Pat, Gino and the rest of the team started to roll out the beautiful, shiny 10-speed bikes for each of our Rwandan "apostles."

When they realized what I was saying they all began to clap, cheer, dance, smile, laugh and hug one another at first, then hugged us as well. I have never seen such sheer joy and happiness having given a gift to anyone in my life.

The cheering, smiling and dancing lasted for several minutes. They all started chanting what we had taught them days earlier... Ole' ole' ole' ole' ole' ole, the soccer chant that became our communication device with these wonderful young men.

At my wife's urging, I then explained who Chase Kowalski was and why bikes were really a gift from him and all the Sandy Hook Angels. I asked if they could say his name. "Chase Kowalski," they repeated.

"Chase Kowalski," our team began to chant over and over and faster and faster, "Chase Kowalski, Chase Kowalski, Chase Kowalski, Chase Kowalski," till we all erupted in applause and hugged and celebrated. It was a moment we never will forget.

Brian McGorty described the scene like an Oprah Winfrey giveaway show, "*You* get a bike, and *you* get a bike, and *you* get a bike!" It was perhaps the most rewarding moment of gift giving I had ever witnessed.

It was clear that as I had hoped, this project was definitely not a gift from us. We were only the caretakers of the gift, it was, in fact, a gift from the Sandy Hook Elementary School Angels and their families and from all the other Where Angels Play Foundation families for whom we advocated for over the years—Hannah, Owen, Lucas, Jesse and so many more of the Angels we felt were with us every step of the way.

We felt a blessing that day and, no doubt we had significantly changed the lives and the economic status of the families of these men. However, we felt like the true beneficiaries of a gift and we had only begun to realize it.

The men jumped onto their new prize possessions and pedaled around the schoolyard as if they had ridden bikes every day of their lives. With an occasional fall and one memorable crash into Brian McGorty, they soon earned their bike skills and were on their way home no doubt eager to share their good fortune with their families.

An emotional day followed by an emotional night of story telling and Mutzig beer and cigars once again somehow acquired by our own Mark Goode. This day set us up for the ribbon cutting ceremony—which would take place along with a very difficult goodbye.

December 1, 2017, was the dedication of the Kibeho, Rwanda playground. Our playground sparkled on a bluff overlooking a magnificent Rwandan meadow. The weather was a picture-perfect 80 degrees. There was a slight breeze but there was not a cloud in the sky. By the time our crew of twenty arrived by bus to the playground and new basketball court, the bluff was filled with perhaps 500 plus children and their families all eager to see what this conglomeration of steel and plastic could possibly mean to their community.

We all gathered together close to the playground surface that was now beautifully landscaped by Jean Paul and the remaining Rwandan "apostles" who chose to stick around and beautify their handiwork. Everyone who had worked on this park took great pride in the splendor including the 20 white American strangers who now stood before an African crowd eager to experience this new wonder.

Through the interpreter, Jean Paul, it was my privilege to tell them all who we were and why we were inspired to build this playground.

I told them the story of Jesse Lewis and his bravery at Sandy Hook. I told them that his brother J.T. was counseled by one of their countrymen and that is why we chose Rwanda as our most recent Where Angels Play Foundation project. I told them that this was a gift from Jesse and Chase and all the Angels who inspire us every day. I further suggested that they should remember their Angels who had gone before them.

I looked over at Yannick with his scar, and Dixon, Robert, Maurice and Charles. I remembered their stories and it was hard to imagine that only two decades earlier this beautiful country ran red with the blood of the genocide. But today was a happy day, not of sadness, grief or death. Today would be a joyous celebration. Today would bring smiles, laughter and the squeals of young voices overwhelmed with gladness.

We cut the ribbon and like no other place we had been, children and adults, young and old, rushed onto the playground with many climbing all over every inch of the structure. You could barely see any steel or plastic through the pulsating mass of humanity that covered their playground... the likes of which had never been seen in this land before.

To further underscore the uniqueness of this playground in Kibeho, the children began to climb through the monkey bars not hanging from or traversing one to the other. They climbed horizontally through each rung with trapeze artists ease. Danny grabbed me to show me how they were climbing and we laughed and marveled at their inventiveness. We thought to try and explain that they were supposed to hang on them versus climb through but we then thought better of it. *Who are we to tell these gymnasts how they should use their new playground?*

We all stood back in awe at the spectacle, so blessed and proud to have been a part of this gift from God.

Brian Dolaghan whispered in my ear, "Bill I loved every playground we built and every ceremony is great, but I gotta say I've never seen a happier sight in my life."

The corkscrew slide seemed to spit out an endless stream of smiling, laughing faces with nonstop joy for hours. Kathy was filmed, crying and laughing at the same time, barely able to stand the emotion. We all cried, laughed, hugged and smiled till our faces hurt. This was a magical moment that would forever be seared in our memories.

We had a few more surprises for the villagers. Before we left for Rwanda I had our team bring suitcases of soccer balls, toys, candy and T-shirts. We began to distribute everything we had. The children and Kibeho villagers were so excited they started to grab and push and pull until one small fight broke out. These folks had so little and they all wanted a piece of the gifts and candy we had brought. While I never felt in any danger and knew that these folks respected and liked us very much, they were starting to become aggressive with each other. Chris McGowan, ever the military professional, thought we needed to leave the gifts and take a step back and for our own safety, allow the candy and goods to be distributed among the villagers as they—not we—saw fit.

With tears in our eyes and lumps in our throats we boarded the bus and listened as the crowd cheered for us, hoping for a last minute gift to be thrown their way. Our members took off their hats, jackets, and even shoes that they could spare and handed them to the ever-ready hands that were reaching into the windows of the bus. The emotions we all felt leaving Kibeho, while watching the crowd and the playground disappear in the distance, cannot be described with the written word. It was heartbreaking and heartwarming all at the same time. We felt a sense of achievement but understood, in reality, so much more was needed. Then I thought of how we all longed to save every child from the harsh realities of life in East Africa.

At that moment, I couldn't help but think of Yannick and his request of medical treatment. I thought of how many times he had been let down. How could we possibly help him and so many others like him? For now, we would have to celebrate our playground and its completion and ponder over what else the Angels might have in store for us.

The Apostles with their gift from Chase

Rebecca Kowalski, responsible for so much Joy, receives token of appreciation

CHAPTER SEVENTEEN

Leaving a Part of Us Behind

With our mission accomplished and new playground and basketball court in place, with a heavy heart we packed up our belongings and said a tearful goodbye to Jean Paul and his amazing team. The "apostles," who had become our family, cried as we left and we all lost it. The bus pulled out and tears flowed. We were exhausted, happy, sad, prayerful and completely overwhelmed. We started to think of our home and our return to the United States.

We hung an American flag in the back of the bus. We made speeches and shared memories. It was somber at first until Brian Dolaghan reminded us that he had one more duffle bag of soccer balls to give out. As we drove across the dirt roads between tea fields and forests we occasionally would see Rwandan children walking along the roadway. Brian, Gino, Kathy, Chris and Shara would take turns throwing the soccer balls to the children. Their reactions were priceless. After they grabbed the ball and realized what it was, an instant grin would flash upon the child's face and they would wave a big thank you. Some looked stunned as if these strange magical balls had fallen out of the sky.

This activity lasted for a good part of the five-hour ride back to Kigali and greatly lightened the mood. Brother Pat sang a song and brother Bob did an impromptu dance in the aisle of the bus.

We headed to Dr. Jim and Gene's house in Kigali for a celebratory barbecue feast. It was a great way to end our Africa journey with the family and friends who had made our trip so enjoyable.

The AKAGERA Production crew interviewed our entire group for final thoughts. One comment or memory was more fascinating than the next. It was clear that every member of our Angels Army was emotionally and spiritually changed by what they had encountered and experienced in this beautiful country. We unanimously agreed that we would never forget the people of Rwanda. They had stolen our hearts and they earned our greatest respect.

Filet mignon on the grill, green beans and potatoes was a delicious good old American meal we all enjoyed. I spoke with Dr. Jim and Gene at length that afternoon and learned about their family and their twin daughters.

Palesa and Caroline were so welcoming and charming and not the least bit shy about meeting our large, sometimes rowdy and loud group of volunteers. They told me of their two older daughters, Ruth and Beth, who were both adopted and now have families of their own.

As I told them how grateful we were for all the help both logistical and cultural—I also let them know how impressed we all were with their family and their film crew. The subject finally rolled around to Yannick and his medical situation. Dr. Jim explained what a bright young man Yannick was, and how he could benefit greatly both physically and psychologically by having his scars treated. Dr. Jim explained that he was working on a possible treatment in Uganda but there were complications and concerns over the quality of treatment Yannick might receive there. I took this all in and stored it for discussion at a later date.

Sean Creighton, Dr. Jim's son, continued his tour guide explanation of things in Kigali and the culture he loved so very much. We learned of the Rwandan sitcom *Mutoni*, Sean and the film crew were working on and how proud they were of it.

The more we spoke to every member of the Creighton family, we realized more and more what remarkable humanitarians they all are. This film crew was talented and so fortunate to be working with Dr. Jim. What a great opportunity they had to try and elevate themselves out of poverty. Before we boarded the bus for the airport we all sang "Sweet Caroline" for Caroline's birthday. This song we were informed held a lot of tradition in the Creighton household whenever guests were coming and going. We all hugged goodbye to our amazing new family—both American and Rwandan—and headed off to the airport for the long journey home.

With a one day stopover in Amsterdam, all 20 of our team had an opportunity to exchange stories, have some much needed rest and relaxation, to catch our proverbial breath and begin to digest all of the wondrous experiences we had just lived through.

Chris and Shara McGowan were not able to stay overnight in Amsterdam, as they had to catch a connecting flight to their home in Kansas City. Before a tearful goodbye, Chris made one of the best speeches to all our troops saying, "Remember, everyone, it is not how often you pray, or how many church visits you make, our measure will be taken by God as to how we impacted the people we encountered, and how much better we leave the people that we visit."

Beautifully stated, it provided the perfect sentiment for us all to travel the remainder of our journey home.

Ray Colavito with his biggest fans

Kibeho Children saying goodbye

CHAPTER EIGHTEEN

God Shed His Grace on Thee

The 20 members of the African Angels Army made their way back to their families and tried to share the many wonderful and life changing experiences with their loved ones. With Mark Goode returning to Orillia, Ontario, and the remaining 19 back in the good ole USA, we counted the many blessings of living in North America—electricity, clean water, plumbing, air conditioning, cars, planes, trains, subways, taxis, fast food, supermarkets, clothes, shoes, and the Jersey Shore.

Many simple pleasures of life brought back memories of all our Rwandan friends and what they didn't have. Too many blessings to mention those that most of us in the western world take for granted were suddenly so starkly evident to each of us as we returned back into our regular every day American or Canadian lives.

The first time I walked into a Dunkin Donuts shop in Penn Station in New York, while changing trains for a trip back from JFK airport I got my first example of how spoiled we are here in America. As I waited in line a woman was handed a cup and realized it was coffee and not the tea as she had ordered,

"Are you kidding me!" she complained. "You people do this all the time. I ordered tea, not coffee. Why can't you get this right? Ridiculous!" she said frowning and complaining.

As the employee behind the counter rolled her eyes and began correcting this "horrible" mistake, I thought to myself, *wow, what a tough life this woman has, and what a hardship to endure being served coffee instead of her expected tea.* My friends back in Kibeho, Rwanda I'm sure could not relate to this sort of difficult problem. I imagine they'd be thrilled with just about anything Dunkin Donuts could offer them.

Back to our families and friends, we all cherished everything and everybody in our lives a little bit more and were a lot more grateful for even the smallest convenience. We had been given a gift of perspective and a new found gratitude for just about everything this big beautiful country of the United States of America has to offer.

Slowly we returned to our regular routines. Some of us went back to work or watching children. In my case I went back to planning playgrounds. The year prior we had built playgrounds for Sean Collier, an M.I.T. police officer who gave his life in the wake of the Boston Marathon bombing. This great project led us to a Boston firefighter named Jimmy Plourde, and Joe Minehan, a fellow burn camp counselor and great member of our Angels Army.

Joe introduced me to Jimmy and we learned of another angel, Victoria McGrath. Jimmy had responded to the Boston Marathon bombing and heroically carried Victoria from the wreckage, saving her from further harm. As Victoria healed, the Plourde family and Victoria became very close, and Jimmy and his wife Michelle considered her family. Sadly about a year after the bombing, Victoria lost her life in a fatal car accident in Dubai during her college spring break. Devastated by the loss of Victoria, Jimmy inquired as to how we could build a playground for Victoria. On April 2, 2016, the Where Angels Play Foundation cut the ribbon on Victoria McGrath's playground at the Dorchester Boy and Girls Club.

Jimmy and his brother firefighters from Boston... Steve, Rohilio, and Joe Minehan became integral parts of the ever-growing Angels Army network. At a fundraising event in Boston for the One World Strong Foundation, my brother Bob, Jimmy and I began talking of all the tragic incidents around the world. When the discussion turned to our recent Africa trip, I told Jimmy about this remarkable young man named Yannick who actually has forgiven his attacker. I was able to show the video interview we had taken of Yannick, and I mentioned that Yannick had asked me if I knew a plastic surgeon who could help him.

Remarkably, Jimmy said, "Believe it or not, my mom works for a great plastic surgeon in Schenectady, New York." He continued, "You know what, it can't hurt for me to ask my mom to mention it to her. Her name is Dr. Fox."

What a coincidence, God wink, or a stroke of great fortune, but if Jimmy could make this connection for us, it would be beyond incredible.

Janet Plourde and her husband Peter, along with Jimmy's Uncle Billy Schmidt were also great members of our Angel Army team, so I knew them well. Jimmy spoke to his mother and she promised to mention Yannick's situation to Dr. Fox and we would see what could happen.

About a week or so later the Where Angels Play Foundation celebrated its five-year anniversary at a great bar and grill on the Jersey Shore called Off the Hook.

Off the Hook served as our New Jersey watering hole for many of the Angels Army get-togethers. It was a great night, almost too great, as the alcohol was going down pretty good and the next morning I wasn't feeling that well. Karen and Joe Burke, great supporters of our foundation, put together a breakfast meeting with Billy Schmidt, Jimmy Plourde's uncle, and Janet and Peter Plourde.

Kathy and I somehow collected ourselves enough to meet at Alice's Restaurant in Sea Bright, New Jersey, the home of our very first playground. Alice, of course, was a great and consistent supporter of the Where Angels Play Foundation as well, so it was a natural spot for us to all get together.

Billy Schmidt a big strong upstate New Yorker, had fit in with our Angels Army gang so well he seemed to always be exactly where we needed him. As we learned at breakfast not only did Janet Plourde work at Dr. Fox's office, but she and Peter and especially Billy were quite good friends with Dr. Fox.

Janet explained that Dr. Fox had, in fact, gone to Africa multiple times to work on children and young Africans with mouth and facial deformities with Partners for World Health. Janet, Peter and Billy thought that Dr. Fox might actually take Yannick on as a patient and asked me for several pictures. I could not believe my ears when I heard that this might happen... another miracle realized.

After a few days my phone rang. The voice on the other end said, "Hello, Bill, this is Pat Fox. I'd like to talk to you about Yannick."

It took me a minute to realize that this was Dr. Patricia Fox the renowned plastic surgeon on the line. She was so down to earth, like talking to the girl next door. She had no airs about her. Dr. Pat Fox was just plain, matter of fact.

She told me, "I saw the picture of your African friend, Yannick, and I'm pretty confident I'll be able to help him. I don't have any trips planned to Africa this year but if you can get him here to me, I'll do the work here at Ellis Hospital."

I almost dropped the phone when she said, "I'll donate my services. There will be no cost for me but you may have to pay some hospital costs, an anesthesia doctor, etc."

I couldn't believe my ears. I thanked her profusely, and she said her office would be in touch. I thanked her again and told her how much this meant to me.

I couldn't wait to call Dr. Jim so he could relay the information to Yannick. Maybe we could make a difference for Yannick after all. Dr. Jim was thrilled and passed the word to Yannick who called me back excitedly and began to cry over the phone. I told him we still had some logistics to take care of but it sure was looking good for this young man to get the medical attention he had been waiting for all his life. I started to realize that this miracle could actually happen and I could almost not believe it myself.

Dr. Jim had planned a trip to the U.S. for June 2018. He wanted to visit his sister Beth and her husband Jack in Shark River, New Jersey, and decided to bring his son Sean along and include Maurice and Robert to continue the filming of their documentary on the Where Angels Play Foundation. They thought it would be great to conclude the film back in our home state of New Jersey.

My nephew, Tim Huber, is a math teacher at North Brunswick High School and he told me that the History Department was studying the Rwandan Genocide. We both thought it would be a great teaching moment for his students to hear directly from Maurice and Robert both genocide survivors. Tim got permission from his principal and put together a program in his high school auditorium to have Maurice and Robert address his students so they could hear first hand what they had experienced and how different life was for so many people in Africa.

The presentation given that day really resonated with the students and faculty. I was able to introduce the mission of the Where Angels Play Foundation and introduce Sean Creighton to represent his Dad, along with Maurice and Robert.

The students really listened intently and were visibly moved by the recollection of the genocide and, in general, how harsh life could be in Africa and how blessed these American high school students were to live in such a wonderful country with so many advantages and opportunities for success.

As I usually do, I ended my talk with my mom's quote, "If you threw your problems in a pile with everyone else's, you would fight to get yours back." I told them I always loved mentioning my mom and told them by mentioning Elizabeth Dwelle Lavin, that is my way to have mom still with me. I also told them they should try and speak about their loved ones who were no longer physically with them, and when they did, they would live on!

I finished that talk by saying that there is usually at least one student or adult who tells me that they felt they were chosen to hear these stories due to the fact they were going through some tough times.

After the talk and while speaking with my nephew and thanking him for putting such a successful event together, he surprised me by saying, "Uncle Bill, I think I was the guy who needed to hear this talk today."

Tim explained that he was struggling with some decisions he was trying to make and wasn't at the happiest juncture in his life but today's presentation really helped him put some things in perspective.

When Tim found out about Yannick's opportunity to come to the U.S., he went even further to help our cause by organizing a "dress down day" fundraiser at the North Brunswick High School. He raised over $1500 to be donated to the Where Angels Play Foundation and off-set the travel costs for Yannick. Needless to say, while I've always been proud of Tim, I was so grateful and never more proud of him than witnessing his commitment to our foundation and Yannick's cause.

Robert, Dr. Jim, Sean and Maurice are welcomed to the USA

CHAPTER NINETEEN

This is America

With Tim Huber and the North Brunswick High School behind us we had the money for the airfare to get Yannick ready for his medical visit to the States. Across the Atlantic Ocean in Rwanda, Dr. Jim was working on the Visa for Yannick and everything appeared to be in place. I had coordinated with Janet Plourde and the team from Dr. Fox's office. Brenda, from Dr. Fox's office, was wonderful in scheduling Yannick for surgery at Ellis Hospital on July 30, 2018. Everything was ready and Dr. Jim had arranged for Yannick to fly out of Kigali to Newark Airport on July 25th. All systems go! Or were they?

On or about July 15th I got a call from Dr. Jim saying that we had a problem. Apparently, Yannick had been arrested for using marijuana earlier in the week and was currently in a jail in Kilgali. UGH!

"You've got to be kidding!" I exclaimed.

After all he's been through and now his dream of coming to America would be postponed for a lousy marijuana arrest. Dr. Jim explained that, if this arrest was documented, it would surely derail his Visa request. I was crushed, angry and disappointed.

If I was devastated by this news, how much more devastated would Yannick be? What was I going to tell Dr. Fox and all the wonderful people who had worked so hard to make this happen?

I decided not to say anything and pray for another miracle to happen. On July 21st I got my miracle. Goretti, Yannick's aunt who worked for law enforcement, had somehow managed to advocate on Yannick's behalf to the authorities and have his record expunged in time for Yannick's Visa to be approved. I learned, much later, about Goretti and Yannick's sometime difficult life while living with Goretti and her husband Peter. I believe, and Yannick later confirmed, he believed as well, that Goretti's work on his behalf was her way of making up for her silence during some abusive treatment at the hand of her husband Peter. Her act of kindness and work on his behalf would ultimately result in a new life and opportunity for Yannick to be made whole somehow. I would love to speak with her someday to confirm that. For now, I was just grateful and thrilled for Yannick to be cleared for travel to the US and his long awaited surgery.

On July 25, 2018, Yannick Kabuguza walked off an Ethiopian Air Lines flight and into the Newark Liberty International Airport. Yannick Kabuguza walked through the line at U.S. Customs and the Customs officer asked, "Why are you here in America, young man?"

Yannick replied, "I have come here to have surgery on my face and ear and have them repaired by a doctor here in America."

The Customs agent looked long and hard at Yannick's face and prominent scar and seemed to take forever as he examined Yannick.

The Customs officer then looked at Yannick's Visa and travel document, banged his stamp hard on them and handed them to Yannick. Yannick started to walk away quietly and then the Customs officer called him back.

Oh no! Yannick thought, *What now?*

The officer looked at Yannick hard once again, then smiled broadly and offered a fist pump to Yannick saying, "Welcome to America, young man and God bless you."

Yannick returned the fist pump and as they touched knuckles, a great sigh of relief came across Yannick and he grinned from ear to ear.

"Thank you, Sir," he smiled and went on his way.

The officer watched Yannick walk through the sign "Welcome to the United States of America," shaking his head while he contemplated what this young man must have gone through to get to this point. He obviously could not have had the slightest clue!

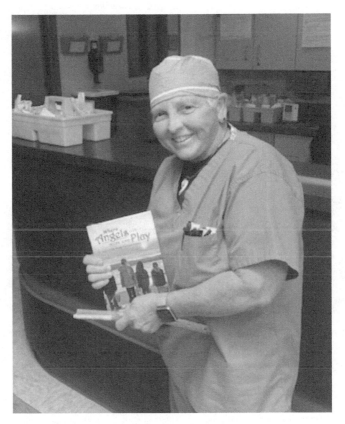

Dr. Patricia Fox ready to read *Where Angels Live, Work and Play*

Billy Schmidt, Peter and Janet Plourde prepare for Yannick's New York visit

CHAPTER TWENTY

Crown Thy Good with Brotherhood

I pulled into the Newark Airport passenger arrival pick up lane. I was hoping to be able to scoop up Yannick quickly so he wouldn't get lost in this strange new country. I waited and waited, a half hour, then an hour, circling the airport, calling him on a number I was given by Dr. Jim. He wasn't answering. I was getting nervous and thought he may have missed the flight or some other way detained.

I finally got a call from him from a strange number and told him where to meet me. After a good hour and half I spotted Yannick walking along the sidewalk of the arrival luggage area. I called him and he looked so surprised and relieved.

He ran to my car and we hugged.

Yannick explained that his phone was not getting any signal and he had to keep asking strangers if he could use their phone to call me. At least five or six people refused or walked away from him until finally some man let him use the phone. He was frantic to get in touch with me, and was finally relieved to see a familiar face. What an ordeal it must've been for Yannick, being in a strange new country, his English wasn't yet the best and he was desperately trying to communicate with me.

When he finally settled down, he began to marvel at my car, which was just a Honda Pilot, but he thought it was a "Umucyrie" car (umucyrie once again in Kinyarwanda means "rich guy"). Yannick was amazed at the traffic, buildings and the highways, as we sped down the New Jersey Turnpike. It was now after 10 p.m. and Yannick told me he was very hungry after the long eighteen-hour flight. It was his first flight and it lasted 18 hours. I could only imagine what he must have been thinking and feeling on his way across the Atlantic Ocean.

I figured I'd go full American on him right away and took him to the Burger Express in Carteret, New Jersey, about two miles from my home. Yannick had two hamburgers, French fries and a coke. He said it was one of the most delicious things he had ever tasted. We had a good laugh about it and headed to Bucknell Avenue in Woodbridge, New Jersey, where I lived with my wife and where we had raised our three children, Charles (Smitty), Kelly and Marykate. We were empty-nesters now, so there was plenty of room for Yannick to stay upstairs with his own bathroom and privacy.

Kathy was waiting for us and she and Yannick enjoyed a great emotional reunion. As we talked into the night none of us could believe Yannick was here in New Jersey and soon would be on his way for surgery in upstate New York.

The next few days we let Yannick ease into life in the suburbs of America. He met Smitty and his wife Dayna, their children Teddy and Juniper; Kelly, my daughter and her husband Billy; and Marykate and her husband Matt and their little five-month old son Matthew.

Yannick enjoyed meeting all the family members and got such a kick out of being able to hold little Matty in his arms. Being so friendly and happy most of the time, Matty gave Yannick a great big smile and Yannick broke out into a hearty laugh. He was so happy whispering to me with great emotion that this was the first white child he was ever permitted to hold. While we thought nothing of it at first, we soon realized the significance that it held for Yannick.

I have six sisters and four brothers so it took a little while before Yannick had a chance to meet them all. Of course, Butch, Pat and Bob were old friends and they spent a good amount of time talking with Yannick throughout his stay. With the surgery on July 30, Yannick had a short time to get the feel of the country, the State of New Jersey, and the Woodbridge community. We made sure he ate good and got plenty of rest for his upcoming medical procedure. Dr. Jim had made sure that all Yannick's pre-admission testing had been completed in Kigali before he had arrived.

We had many friends and family coming and going the first few days of Yannick's stay. On July 28th a friend of mine stopped over our house. This visit would prove to be life changing, not only for him, but also for Yannick for years to come.

Matt Mitrow is a great friend of mine, whom I had met while I was president of the NJ Fireman's Mutual Benevolent Association. Matt and his brother Michael had built a company from the ground up. Representing pharmaceutical companies and using their marketing skills they helped to educate the public about high blood pressure, heart disease and COPD, Matt and Michael created a small niche for themselves among labor unions.

With the help of Matt and Mike Mitrow the NJFMBA was able to provide health screening of our members free of charge while at the same time providing information on whatever brand of corrective medicine was recommended on behalf of the participating pharmaceutical corporation. Getting a health screening for the many risks firefighters face was of utmost importance to our membership. The extra benefit was that Matt, in particular, always supported the many charities of the NJ FMBA. Breast Cancer, Fallen Heroes Fund, 9/11 Memorial causes and the Where Angels Play Foundation all benefitted from their support.

In fact, part of the reason I had the confidence to start the Where Angels Play Foundation was due to the consistent support I could count on from Matt and Michael Mitrow.

Matt became part of my family. He loved a party and always was over the top to celebrate a special day, or achievement of the firefighters, Where Angels Play, or our sons and daughters.

His humanitarian efforts extended to the Children's Ward of the Memorial Sloan Kettering Cancer Treatment Center. Matt, his wife and kids would join me at Christmas time to bring gifts to the young cancer patients at Sloan. Matt and Rae Marie Mitrow entertained the

Noble family in Walt Disney World and treated them like royalty. Jeff and Connie Noble from Orillia, Ontario, were scheduled to take their children, Jacob, Kayleigh and Kaden to Disney with the Make a Wish Foundation. Unfortunately when Jacob Noble lost his battle with a debilitating disease, the trip was cancelled. The Where Angels Play Foundation decided that wasn't fair to Kayleigh and Kaden. So, with the help of Matt and Rae Marie, a vacation of a lifetime was provided for them. Matt and Rae Marie were known for doing such beautiful things for many.

Matt and Rae Marie's children, Abby, Ben and Macey, also benefitted greatly from their exposure to, and work on behalf of, the the Where Angels Play Foundation. The kids learned empathy and compassion for others, and how not to take things for granted. Ben even chose the number 26 on his football jersey to honor the 26 Angels from the Sandy Hook Elementary School. The Mitrow family thought little of these charitable deeds, believing I guess, they were just the right things to do. After all, business was good and life was great for Team Mitrow!

But life is never perfect or easy, and soon some sobering realities hit Matt and his business. The economy eventually took a turn for the worse, and business was not as good as it used to be, and the growth of Matt's company stagnated.

Matt was carrying the weight of the world on his shoulders now, and he wasn't the least bit happy about it. Everything had been going so smooth, and he had been so kind to so many, and now, life suddenly didn't seem fair.

Just before my trip to Africa, Ken Burkert, another great friend of both Matt and I, called me to have a heart-to-heart meeting with Matt. We were both worried about Matt, and if he continued down this path of depression and self-loathing, he could lose it all.

After some tough love and sobering advice, we were able to convince Matt that he, by all measures had a great life, a great wife and great kids. He needed to celebrate what he had achieved. He needed to address his problems (both personal and financial) and pull it all together.

Matt realized he needed to take stock of his life and stop feeling sorry for himself, and just be happy again and joyful again to celebrate the only things that were important—his family and his friends. Basically, Matt needed my mom's advice... Betty Lavin would say, "Throw your problems in a pile with everyone else, and you'll fight to get yours back." And so Matt did! He began a new attitude and a new life for himself.

Meeting Yannick at my house on this Friday afternoon was perfect timing, not only for Yannick, but also for Matt as well. When I introduced Yannick to Matt, I explained about his face and ear and exactly how that had happened, the life he lived and the tragedy he'd lived through. I explained to Matt the miracles that had brought him here to the United States and the surgery that awaited him in New York. Of course Yannick's decision to forgive his attackers, was almost, too much for Matt to comprehend.

Matt looked at me with astonishment and I saw a visible change in him. It was as if Matt was thinking...*and I thought I had problems?*

I believe Matt decided there and then that he would never complain about his life ever again. Matt also decided that he could help this kid. He was determined to do whatever he could, to make Yannick's life better, and wanted a part of changing Yannick's reality.

Matt said, "This kid is due for some breaks, and I'm gonna try and make them happen."

Yannick liked Matt as well, and was grateful for him wanting to help him, but I do not think Yannick really believed that Matt would really take an interest in him. Little did Yannick realize, the blessing of a man that Matt Mitrow was about to be. Yannick's life would never be the same.

Yannick in the shadow of Lady Liberty

Yannick's first experience at the Jersey Shore with Bill and his sister Joyce

CHAPTER TWENTY-ONE

God Mend Thine Every Flaw

The last couple of days before the operation were filled with long conversation with Yannick about his trip to the United States. We spoke of how he almost blew his chances for freedom and a new life for the sake of smoking marijuana. Yannick explained that as a teenager he would use marijuana as a painkiller and as an escape from his personal pain... being trapped behind his scar. Yannick felt that he was branded a victim and he wore his scar as a scarlet letter.

Yannick believed he would be defined by his facial wounds.

He explained, that his jail cell window was close enough to the Kigali International Airport. He watched the jet planes leaving everyday and cried as he imagined all those passengers leaving for America and thought he had ruined his chances of ever leaving Rwanda.

Yannick was mixed in with every thief, murderer and rapist that called his jail cell home. He spoke respectfully of Goretti and his gratitude for her kind deeds in securing his freedom and facilitating his records needed to pave the way for a medical visa to the United States. Yannick spoke again of forgiveness toward Peter and how difficult he had made his childhood but now had found God and salvation.

Then he looked at me, with a broad grin and said, "But look at me now, I am here in America, a dream come true." He continued, "I will never be able to thank you, Kathy and all the Where Angels Play Foundation."

I assured Yannick that we were honored to have him live with us and privileged to witness his upcoming surgery, and hopefully, watching all his dreams coming true.

We traveled the three and one half hours, from Woodbridge, NJ, to Schenectady, NY, where a dinner was planned to meet with Billy Schmidt, Peter and Janet Plourde, and Dr. Patricia Fox for the very first time.

Dr. Jim Creighton flew in from Africa to surprise us and told Yannick he would be able to scrub in and be there for him for his surgery. Dr. Jim's presence put Yannick at much greater ease.

Janet, Peter and Billy welcomed Yannick and were excited and thrilled to meet him. Dr. Fox arrived and her presence filled up the room. She was short in stature and long on personality. Dr. Fox is quick-witted, confident, and intelligent and was also knowledgeable about Africa, Rwanda in particular, and the genocide. She seemed eager for the challenge of repairing Yannick's ear and cheek.

She was full of energy and enthusiasm for all things. Dr. Fox could talk sports, politics or construction and was a brilliant renowned surgeon who drove a Ford F-250. A joy to be around, Dr. Fox put Yannick at ease and spoke matter of factly about how she would snip this and pull that and how this operation would be a routine "walk in the park." Not really, but she made Yannick confident that he was in the best possible hands.

Dr. Fox had informed us that Yannick's face and ear had healed by "secondary intent," meaning it was never sewn or stitched together. Over years it had just closed up on its own in the position that was driven by gravity and not medicine.

The dinner ended with Dr. Fox taking some pictures of Yannick's face, and then some photos of all of us together. Photography was just another discipline of Dr. Fox in which she was quite skilled and knowledgeable. Then we left to prepare and rest for the next day surgery. Dr. Jim, Yannick, and I stayed together in a nearby hotel and spoke about all the things that had to go just right in order for this next day surgery to take place. We all felt that divine intervention had to be involved.

I believed with all my heart that God was directing Yannick now and this surgery would go well. Yannick was understandably nervous, and it showed.

All the excitement and the realization that Yannick was about to have major surgery on his face and ear started to sink in. I'm sure none of us got much sleep that night, especially Yannick.

The next day at 6:00 a.m., we traveled together for Yannick's prep and eventual surgery. Dr. Fox allowed Dr. Jim to scrub in and he was able to film parts of the operation with his phone for me to view later. Not an easy watch, I was amazed at the brilliant artistry of Dr. Fox's handiwork. She had music playing in the background and talked through the entire operation to keep herself relaxed. It was like watching poetry in motion.

Dr. Jim and Dr. Fox came out to the waiting room to tell me that everything had gone beautifully. Dr. Fox seemed pleased, almost excited, that she was able to re-attach Yannick's ear and was confident the scars on his face and ear would be minimal at the very worst, and promised to "touch him up," if ever the need should arise.

Dr. Fox also surprised me when she said that the anesthesiologist had waived his fee for Yannick's operation, as did the Ellis Hospital.

Remarkably, she simply stated, "There will be no bill!"

"Wow, Unbelievable!" I said.

Yannick's dream was coming true, and so many people wanted a hand in making it happen. I gave Dr. Fox a big hug and thanked her with tears flowing. Dr. Jim too was thrilled. What a brilliant and talented human being Dr Fox is, and she was so kind and humble, as well. I know, she knew, she was giving Yannick a new lease on life and her satisfaction was quite evident.

About an hour later I was able to see Yannick. His face and head were heavily bandaged but he was in good spirits. He would not be able to eat solid food for at least 12 hours. We celebrated with his now favorite snack... milk shakes and McFlurries from McDonalds.

Dr. Jim, Billy Schmidt and I took Yannick back to the room for his recovery and a quiet night's sleep. I couldn't believe he was allowed to leave the hospital in only twelve hours but then again we did have Dr. Jim with us as Yannick's private physician just in case anything went wrong.

Yannick, had a tough night when the anesthesia wore off. We tried to keep him comfortable with Tylenol and Codeine but he was extremely uncomfortable which Dr. Fox told us to expect.

Dr. Jim trained me on how to change Yannick's bandages and how to keep the wound clean etc. The next morning we headed back to New Jersey. Yannick's healing—both physically and emotionally—would now begin.

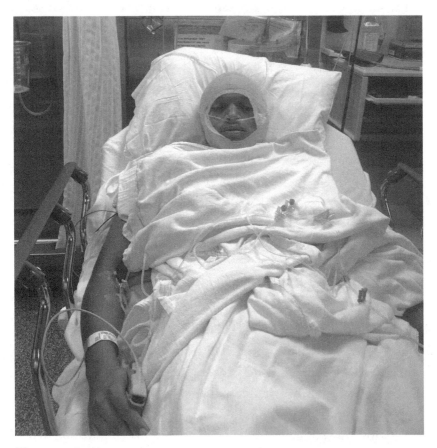

The operation is a success

Yannick enjoys a McFlurry

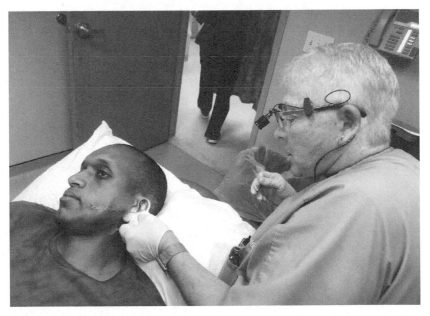

Dr Fox removes Yannick's stitches

CHAPTER TWENTY-TWO

Slow by Slow

"How are you feeling, Yannick?" Kathy or I would ask. "A little better, slow by slow," Yannick would reply.

Each time we asked the same question over the next few weeks, Yannick would reply, "Slow by slow, a little better each day."

"Slow by slow" would actually become sort of his battle cry.

When Billy Schmidt would call and ask, "How is slow by slow doing today?"

The answer was always the same, "Slow by slow." And then he would laugh.

While changing his bandages, I got a peek at Yannick's face and ear. His ear was whole, no longer split in half, and the thick, dark, broad line on his face was now as thin as a pencil mark.

Incredible, I thought to myself. Each day Yannick caught a glimpse of himself in the mirror he was a bit more confident and certainly very happy.

We couldn't wait to show him off to everyone, but he needed to heal and get well. He needed to digest all that had happened to him. Kathy would cook her specialty meals for Yannick—bacon and eggs in the morning—meatballs and spaghetti, chicken parmesan, roasted chicken and of course Yannick's favorite, cheeseburgers. Yannick was eating well, feeling better each day and becoming more and more at home in Woodbridge, New Jersey.

Two weeks after Yannick's surgery we traveled back to Dr. Fox's office to have his stitches removed. Dr. Fox was thrilled with her work and commented that Yannick looked even better than she had hoped.

Without the stitches Yannick looked amazing, still red and swollen, but you could see he was on his way to a complete facial makeover.

Billy Schmidt met us for lunch afterwards. He and I joked about being broken-down-horse-players and decided we were not so far away from Saratoga Racetrack, and it would be a cool place for Yannick to experience a beautiful setting in the Saratoga Springs resort area.

We thanked Dr. Fox again for her gracious service and did a quick press conference with the administrators of Ellis Hospital who had also been so kind to Yannick. We then headed off to Saratoga Racetrack to bet a few races, even though my wife thought I was crazy.

As soon as we got there I started searching the program for hunches, maybe a name like African survivor, Yannick's Dream, or something about surgery. There were some names we bet on but of course none of them won.

We were discussing our losses and I suddenly realized, "Wait a minute, Yannick had a nickname in Rwanda for winning the soccer MVP, Mr. Number One!" I shouted.

Of course, we should have been playing the number one horse the whole time. This is how my crazy horse-playing mind works.

So I told Yannick I would bet the number one horse for him and off I went to the betting window. Well just before I could get a bet placed, the bell goes off and the race starts. That's called "getting shut out," in gamblers jargon! Before I can get back to Billy and Yannick the horses are coming down the stretch and, of course, number one is in the lead. I look at the odds on number one and it is 20–1.

Oh my goodness, wouldn't you know it, I think to myself. Yannick now is so excited that number one wins. I don't have the heart to tell him, I didn't place the bet. He was so happy, jumping up and down. I couldn't tell him the truth.

"How much did I win?" He said.

"$100 dollars!" I say.

He nearly lost his mind, as $100 American currency in Rwandan franks is $120,000.

We all laughed and celebrated but, because now I'm out $100, I think to myself, *Come on, God, throw me a bone here!* I put a good amount of money on number one the next race and sure enough it won again. Mr. Number One wins again!

This time it paid $12.00 to win but I more than recouped my losses on the Yannick "win!"

Billy and I had a good laugh with Yannick that day.

At one point, Yannick said, "Do you mean people actually throw their money away betting on these horses?"

I thought long and hard about that question.

"Yeah I guess it is pretty stupid!" I had to admit.

That was not the first or last observation Yannick would make to teach me about some things in America I routinely took for granted. After a few drinks, great meal, and a lot more laughs, we said goodbye to Billy Schmidt and thanked him for all he had done for Yannick. We told him we would see him at the next playground build and back to New Jersey we went.

On the ride home, Yannick asked me a question that would change the course of our relationship and would begin the thought process that would alter Yannick's future drastically.

"Hey Bill, why do I have to go back to Rwanda?" Yannick asked.

This caught me off guard.

Yannick was scheduled to fly back to Kigali, Rwanda at the end of August, only two weeks away.

"What do you mean, Yannick, you mean you want to stay here in America?" I asked.

"Hell yeah," he said.

"Really? For how long were you thinking?" I responded.

"Forever!" he exclaimed with a big smile.

I wasn't sure if he was joking. *What if he wasn't?* My mind raced.
Where would he live, with me, and for how long?
Where would he work or go to school?
Hmmm

I think he's serious, I thought!

"What about your family in Rwanda?" I asked,

I obviously was not thinking that question through.

Yannick replied, "I really don't have family in Rwanda except for Dr. Jim, Gene, Sean and the girls but they are not my real family."

I replied, "What about Christmas, birthdays, holidays?"

Yannick laughed out loud and said, "What are you talking about, Bill. I never celebrate Christmas or birthdays. I don't even know when my birthday is."

I responded, incredulously, "Come on, Yannick, are you kidding me? You never had a birthday party with cake and people giving you gifts?"

Yannick laughed harder, "No such thing for me in Rwanda, Bill," he said.

I was silent and shocked, trying to imagine his life, no Christmas, no birthdays, no holiday dinners!

How sad, I thought, and I realized at that moment that Yannick was serious. He really wanted to stay right here in America, and forever! *But how?*

Mr. Number One at Saratoga

CHAPTER TWENTY-THREE

It Must Have Been God's Plan

Dr. Jim scheduled a lunch for us at restaurant in Bradley Beach, a town on the New Jersey shore. We would be meeting his sister, Beth, and her husband Jack. Beth and Jack were two great people. Beth was a former schoolteacher, and Jack was a retired Jersey City Police Detective. Yannick, Kathy, Marykate, my daughter, Director of the Where Angels Play Foundation, and I all met at an Italian restaurant, called Uva Pagano, along with Dr. Jim.

Beth had met Yannick on a previous trip to Rwanda while visiting Dr. Jim and his family. Beth was so thrilled about Yannick's good fortune and freshly repaired face. Not that we didn't think he was handsome before but now with his ear restored and scar removed we joked that he was now better looking than Denzel Washington. He would always get a good laugh when we called him "Denzel." But he actually preferred to be called "slow by slow."

Beth told me a story about how she knew of the Where Angels Play Foundation, back in November 2013, when we were building a playground in Belmar. Beth explained that she taught at the same school in Brielle, New Jersey, with my niece, Jackie Adase. Jackie was our chairperson for the Belmar playground celebrating the life of Avielle Richman, an Angel from Sandy Hook Elementary School. Not only had Beth bought T-shirts celebrating our foundation from Jackie, she had sent them to Dr. Jim, Gene and the kids when they were living in Nicaragua.

I was amazed to find out that they were the very shirts Dr. Jim and Gene were wearing when they met us at the airport in Kigali back in November, 2017. I couldn't believe the full circle connection to the

Creighton clan and the Where Angels Play Foundation. Dr. Jim, Gene and the kids were wearing our foundation shirts years before they knew anything about us. Incredible!

This story screamed to me that every step of our journey to Africa was preordained by a higher power. This was just another amazing sign that we were destined to go to Africa to build in Kibeho and ultimately, meet Yannick. It was as if this was all planned out for us and for him. Needless to say, we had a great celebration lunch with Beth and Jack. They are still like family today to Yannick and to us as well.

Kathy hosts Beth and Jack Creighton along with Robert, Maurice and Sean

CHAPTER TWENTY-FOUR

The Student becomes the Teacher

The N.A.G.E. Convention:

One of the Where Angels Play Foundation's most loyal and consistent supporters is the National Association of Government Employees or N.A.G.E. I have had the honor of serving on the N.A.G.E. executive board for the past 15 years. N.A.G.E. is a powerful advocate for civil servants and working families all across America. They are led by an incredible group of people whom I have grown to love like family.

The leader of this robust organization is David Holway who has been the N.A.G.E. president for as long as I've been involved.

Ever since we founded the Where Angels Play Foundation, David Holway and N.A.G.E. have generously supported us with their time and financial contributions through the amazing charitable arm of their organization called N.A.G.E. Charities, led by Mary Sheehan and John Mann.

One convention I was unable to attend I actually had the opportunity to Skype my report from Kibeho, Rwanda to keep my union brothers and sisters informed of how their contributions were being used on the other side of the world.

The September, 2018, N.A.G.E. convention was held at the Golden Nugget Hotel and Casino in Atlantic City, New Jersey. This was only six weeks after Yannick's surgery. David Holway invited me to give a report on the Where Angels Play Foundation and asked if I could bring Yannick to tell his story as well. I thought this would be a great opportunity for our N.A.G.E. members to meet Yannick as well as a great opportunity for Yannick to share his story.

On September 13, 2018, I introduced Yannick on the convention floor of N.A.G.E. and briefly told his story of pain and suffering, as well as, and more importantly his narrative of success and forgiveness.

When Yannick addressed the group one could hear a pin drop. It was so quiet.

Yannick told his version of the "Starfish on the Beach" story and the audience loved it. Yannick ended his talk by saying the following, "Some of you may have had an argument or disagreement with someone here, or you may feel someone at home has done you wrong." He continued, "Do yourself a favor and forgive them. It will be a gift to yourself and you will feel so much better."

Yannick ended his talk with this question, "If I can forgive the soldiers who killed my family and scarred my face for life, how much easier will it be for you to forgive somebody who has done much less to you?"

The crowd rose to their feet and gave Yannick a thunderous standing ovation.

As Yannick and I left the dais, Gina Lightfoot Walker, the lead N.A.G.E. attorney said to me through tears, "I love you for bringing that young man here today. He is exactly what we all needed right now."

After the meeting, Yannick was surrounded by many of the N.A.G.E. members... some wanted to hug him, shake his hand and thank him for his beautiful message. There was a line twenty deep and it took a half hour before Yannick finished receiving all the heartfelt expressions of support.

As we left the room, one great friend of mine on the executive board called me aside to speak to me. He was crying and very emotional. "You know that young man just changed my life," he said.

"What do you mean?" I asked.

He explained, "President Holway was very angry at me due to a misunderstanding regarding a statement I had made during a N.A.G.E. executive board meeting." He continued, "I meant no harm but it was taken the wrong way." Apparently this board member had been removed from his appointment on the board because of this perceived offense.

The gentlemen continued to explain, "After listening to Yannick speak about forgiveness, President Holway said to me, 'If Yannick can forgive after all he's been through, then certainly I can forgive you. I'd like to reappoint you to the board and all is forgiven.'"

What a remarkable turn of events I thought. Yannick's story and example of forgiveness had instant impact on this leader and the executive board. I later confirmed the story with David and he admitted how much he was moved by Yannick's story.

Yannick was so amazed and thrilled that he could have such an influence on these impressive important American men. I remember considering his impact on the world was just beginning.

The next day President David Holway presented Yannick with an Honorary Membership Card and a check for his speaking fee. Yannick was speechless and could not believe the extent to which he was welcomed by such an important labor organization.

Months later Yannick would use his membership card from N.A.G.E. as one form of identification at the New Jersey Motor Vehicles Division in order to receive his New Jersey driver's permit and license.

In the wake of Yannick's speaking success, a thought occurred to me about Heather Waters, who had been a friend and a fellow burn camp counselor. She was a teacher at Scarsdale High School in New York. Heather had asked me in the past to speak to her students about the Where Angels Play Foundation and the Children's Burn Camp. The school was just magnificent. It looked like an old castle and was situated in a very wealthy suburb of New York. The students there were brilliant and had every chance for great success. I think the vast majority of graduates of Scarsdale High School eventually attend Ivy League schools or impressive universities around the country.

Heather had arranged another opportunity for me to engage the kids at Scarsdale High. I was excited this time to bring Yannick and have him speak to these great kids.

When we arrived the morning of our talk at Scarsdale High School, Yannick was amazed at the beautiful homes in the area and the structure of the school. He said it looked like a castle from a fairy tale he had seen once on TV. We assembled in a large auditorium. The students and teachers packed the room to where there was standing room only. I introduced Yannick. He was nervous at first but then he hit his stride and told his amazing story of survival and how he felt great joy in being able to come to the United States. He commented how incredible it was to imagine that each of the students seemed to have their own car. Not just any car but he noticed Mercedes Benz, Lexus, Jaguar, Porsche etc. in the parking lot. .

He said, "You are all so very lucky to live in such a great country, I would kiss the ground if I lived here in America."

Yannick took some questions about his country and what it was like to live in Rwanda today. What was the economy like? Was the war still going on?

Then one very bright insightful young student asked Yannick, "I know we have a lot here in the U.S. that unfortunately you do not have in Africa. Can you tell me, what is it that you might have there, that we do not have here in America?"

Yannick smiled and laughed to himself a little as he hesitated to answer. "If I'm going to be honest," he said, "appreciation."

A hush came over the room and the teachers and students began to nod their heads in the affirmative while looking at one another. Murmurs echoed through the hall, then silence, then the room exploded with applause. All the students and teachers rose to their feet and applauded for Yannick. The message they received that day was priceless. Heather and her fellow teachers thanked us and told me that Yannick's message is exactly what these students needed to hear, one word, very simply stated... "Appreciation!"

It was moments like this that had me come to the realization that it really was Yannick who could teach us, rather than the other way around. He had so much to learn, but he also had so much to teach without even realizing it.

While Yannick was living with Kathy and me in Woodbridge we had many conversations about his past life in Rwanda. He explained that there really wasn't much waiting for him back in Kigali. Of course he had the job with Dr. Jim, but he knew that that was only temporary. The more we got to know Yannick the more we realized how extremely intelligent he was. For instance Yannick knew five languages when he arrived here in America. They are Kinyarwanda, his native tongue, Swahili, French, English and a little bit of German. Yannick's English was improving every day and he was healing and his face was looking better each passing day.

Yannick was so curious about everything in America—our culture, slang, what things meant, and cost. Yannick wondered why I owned two houses? He was referring to the garage that I had turned into a "man cave" as well as my small, expanded Cape Cod-style house. We laughed at that but it really gave us a sense of appreciation for all the things we're blessed to have.

Yannick marveled at the fact that every person he met who was old enough to drive had their own car. This was such a foreign concept to him. Owning a car in Rwanda means you are wealthy beyond imagination. We filled the days with meeting more family members and friends. I loved showing off my new African friend to everyone I knew. For me, Yannick was a living, breathing miracle.

We had the great opportunity to have Yannick visit North Brunswick High School. My nephew Tim Huber and his students had been so supportive of Yannick and had raised the money to offset his travel expenses.

We were able to introduce Yannick to Beth Passner, the amazing History teacher, who had helped arrange the presentation of Maurice and Robert the year before. Beth Passners' teaching of the Rwandan Genocide inspired her students, and changed their lives no doubt.

Now Beth, Tim and students from North Brunswick High School were getting to meet the man whose life they had impacted so significantly. What a great teaching moment for all involved, I thought.

Yannick's message of forgiveness and triumph over tragedy was a gift to anyone who would be lucky enough to hear it.

Yannick visits Tim Huber at North Brunswick High

CHAPTER TWENTY-FIVE

An American Birthday

It was becoming increasingly clear that Yannick wanted desperately to stay in America. It was obvious that some of the natural concerns I had for Yannick regarding missing holidays and birthdays were completely moot. I had to wrap my head around the fact that Yannick didn't receive birthday presents. Not just one or two years that Yannick's birthday was somehow forgotten, but always forgotten. Imagine, I thought, never having a birthday party in your life. Imagine never receiving a birthday present ever!

I thought of some birthdays when I was young, when I didn't quite get the exact bike I wanted or the game I wanted or the trip I wanted. I remember being upset at someone close to me when they may have forgotten to call on my birthday. I thought of my kids and grandkids who may have been disappointed from time to time by only getting ten or twelve presents and maybe not the exact one they had really wanted.

No birthday party, no birthday cake, no presents, no birthday cards in the mail and no surprises ever! Imagine, I really could not!!

Yannick actually told me that because of the genocide he didn't even know the actual date of his real birthday. He had no birth certificate due to the fact all the records were destroyed in the war. The birthdate that he was using on his passport was completely fabricated.

The Where Angels Play Foundation was working on a playground build in Lavallette, New Jersey, in mid September. The build was for a remarkable young man, Brendan Tevlin, the grandson of a close friend and NJFMBA legend, Tom Tevlin. Brendan lost his life in a senseless domestic terrorist attack.

We were all excited to work with the Tevlin family to try and bring some joy to them. I asked Yannick to attend the build and witness the "Angels Army" team at their absolute best. Yannick was eager to help and be physically involved with the completion of a playground on U.S. soil.

I was happy to introduce Yannick to Brendan's family, especially his brother, Sean, and his friends from Seton Hall Prep. I had an opportunity to tell them all about Yannick's story of survival and forgiveness. I could see it had a profound effect on the Tevlin family.

I had an idea to surprise Yannick for the first time in his life the evening after the playground was completed. At the volunteer firehouse that hosted a great celebratory dinner for us I decided we would have a birthday cake and sing to Yannick. We figured out that Yannik would probably be about 28 years old, so we chose the 28th of September to celebrate his birthday.

Days earlier, I had e-mailed the "Angels Army" to try and bring some birthday presents to Yannick that night if possible.

After a great dinner hosted by Councilwoman Anita Zalom, I asked for everyone's attention. I asked them to imagine having your birthday be forgotten—not this year but every year. I then asked Yannick to come to the front of the room. He had no idea what I was talking about to the rest of the crowd. I then asked everyone to join me in singing the "Lavin version" (which is 5 songs long) of Happy Birthday to Yannick Kabuguza.

As everyone began to sing Nancy Ur rolled out a large sheet cake glowing with 28 lit candles. The cake read "Happy 28th Birthday Yannick" and was decorated with American flags and Rwandan flags, symbolizing his birth country and his new country. As the crowd boomed the Happy Birthday song Yannick's eyes were wide open, he began to nervously laugh, and as the song morphed into, "For he's a jolly good fellow," Yannick broke down and cried. I had my arm around him and felt his whole body tremble as he could not stop shaking and crying. After the last song of the "Lavin version" of Happy Birthday, Grand Old

Flag was sung. Yannick thanked me and hugged Nancy and started to walk away to thunderous applause of the crowd.

"Wait Yannick," I said.

"You forgot to blow out the candles," I told him.

"Why do I have to do that? Will it cause a fire?" Yannick asked.

"No, it is tradition, my friend, everyone has to blow out the candles on their birthday cake," I said.

"Oh okay, I'm sorry for that, I didn't know," he said through tears.

I thought to myself, *my God, he wasn't even aware he needed to blow out the candles on his cake!*

The wonderful gang of the "Angels Army" never let me down and surrounded Yannick with birthday presents.

The following generous members gave Yannick the best first birthday ever: Mary Ann, Dan, Toni, Rich, Nancy, John, Debbie, Denise, John, Karen, Connor, Billy, Elaina, Brian, Lorri, Joyce, Mike, Jackie, Matt, Rae Marie, Monique, Sue, John, Robbie,Craig, Laura, Josh, Tommy, Jesse, Brian, Richie, Mike, Bob, Greg and of course Kathy, Marykate, Matt, Kelly, Billy and little Matty.

Tom Tevlin made a great speech thanking the entire team and wishing Yannick the happiest birthday ever.

This was not a regular birthday celebration. This was America wishing Yannick 28 Happy Birthdays he had previously never had. Any one who was there that evening received a gift of perspective we could not have gotten anywhere else in the world. We all left hoping Yannick would never have another birthday that was ever forgotten.

When the night ended Yannick told me that from now on his birthday would be celebrated on this day the 28th of September.

With a great big smile, Yannick said to me, "This is America!"

Nancy Ur celebrates Yannick's birthday

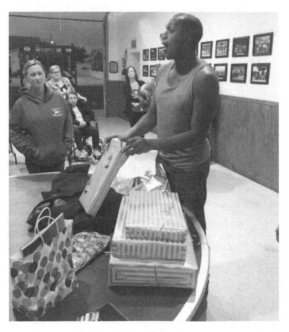

Marykate, Kelly and Matty look on as Yannick
opens his very first birthday present!

CHAPTER TWENTY-SIX

Send These, the Homeless Tempest-tost to me

When the time drew near for Yannick's return flight to Africa he began to grow quiet and reserved. He was always polite and appreciative of everything we had been able to do for him. One day about a week before Yannick was set to fly back to Kigali, Matt Mitrow came by to have lunch with Yannick and me. Matt was really doing well, he had quit drinking and was working out. He looked great and he was back to being the happy, personable, life of the party sort of guy, that we knew and loved. He was appreciating his family and seemed to be clicking on all cylinders with his business once again.

It was his attitude, however, that was really what made me happy for him. He was no longer feeling sorry for himself but rather, was taking it "slow by slow," as Yannick would say. Matt rolled up his sleeve and showed me a new tattoo he had engraved on his arm: " SLOW by SLOW" it read. Yannick and I laughed almost in disbelief. That was a great example, I thought, of the kind of impact Yannick was having on Matt and so many others. Yannick shook his head in amazement.

We spoke with Matt about Yannick's future and how he now had a new lease on life. Yannick mentioned he really would prefer to stay here in America but time was running short.

Matt said matter of fact, "Yannick, you want to stay?" He yelled, "Then why the hell don't you stay?"

"Hey Bill," Matt asked, "What has to happen in order for Yannick to stay?"

"Well, it's complicated," I explained.

I went on in detail that Yannick was here on a medical visa and that would expire soon unless we got it extended.

Matt shouted, "F**kin ' A!" Which was Matt's favorite reply to almost anything he agreed with. "Let me check with my attorney and see what we could do," he said.

Yannick and I asked Matt if he was serious and he replied once again even louder, "F**kin ' A!"

We laughed again and had a great lunch. The next day I had a serious talk with Matt about Yannick's status. He assured me he would find the best immigration attorney in New York and see what we could do for Yannick.

Matt went on to tell me that he had come to realize a lot of things over the course of the last month while working his way out of depression.

He said, "I've had a great life and sometimes didn't realize it." He continued, "I threw a lot of money away on a lot of nothing, just excess food and drink and gifts that most people didn't appreciate."

"You know what Bill? This kid needs help and if I'm in a position to help him then it will be money much better spent than almost anything else I could have done with it."

"Alright," I said. "If you're willing to help finance some of this stuff for him, I'll try and make it happen and we'll figure it out together."

"F**kin ' A," he said once again, and we laughed.

I knew at that moment that I had a willing partner to help me further Yannick's stay here in America. I did wonder how it would all play out and was nervous about this awesome responsibility of having Yannick remain in the states.

Would he continue to live with me? If so, for how long? Where would he work? Would he go to school? How would he adapt to American life? How would Yannick deal with things like racism? Social interaction? Navigating transportation?

There was so much for Yannick to learn about America. His culture is so different. At times it was like he dropped from outer space into a strange new world.

What about health care? a driver's license? Money? Food? Everything you could imagine had to be explained to him.

To say I was nervous about it would be an understatement. Some how it felt right and with Matt as a remarkable resource, I believed that I would figure it out. Kathy was unbelievably supportive and felt like since we had come this far, why not try to give Yannick a much better life than he ever dreamt.

When I would discuss these things with Yannick I often told him we would have to check with the "boss" meaning Kathy. It wasn't long before Yannick began referencing Kathy as the "boss."

"What's the 'boss' think?" he would say. Or "How's the 'boss' to-day?" We all would laugh every time.

During the time Yannick lived with us in Woodbridge he was always willing to help.

I was doing some work on the "man cave," and painting the back room and his room upstairs. He was a quick learner, strong and always full of energy.

He felt the need to do some chores and sort of earn his keep. He had a great work ethic, very similar to our buddies, the "apostles", we had met in Kibeho.

Matt reached out with a name of an attorney from Manhattan. Her name was Alexandra Tsietlin. Yannick, Matt and I took the train over to meet with her and discuss his chances of staying. After hearing Yannick's story, Alexandra told us she felt his best chance to stay was with an application for asylum, which is a process by which a person applied for residence here in the States due to political or civil unrest.

We felt Yannick's case certainly qualified for asylum as he had been through the most difficult time. We were reminded that there were millions of people, "refugees," just like Yannick who were looking for the same entrance into this country and a new life in the land of opportunity known as the United States of America. Alexandra explained to me that she herself was a refugee and had come from the Ukraine, so she could relate very well to Yannick's plight.

While she couldn't promise anything, she would do her very best to win asylum for Yannick Kabuguza. Matt agreed to hire Alexandra and generously cover all the legal expenses for an attempt at winning asylum for Yannick.

Alexandra explained to us that Yannick's medical visa was actually good for six months. So we had until at least January 25th to try to get a new visa or perhaps get a decision on his asylum status. Now it was decided Yannick would stay for at least six months and a lot would have to be arranged.

Matt suggested that Kathy and I could use a little help in taking care of Yannick. Matt was willing to find an apartment for Yannick to stay at least for the time being.

After a brief hotel stay in Westfield, Matt and his wife, Rae Marie, found a studio apartment for Yannick on Hamilton Street in Rahway, New Jersey. Yannick often visited with Rae Marie, Matt and their three great kids, Abby, Ben and Macey. The Mitrow kids grew fascinated by Yannick, his accent and good-naturedness. Rae Marie would often have Yannick over for dinner and he now became a part of the Mitrow family.

When Yannick's apartment was ready to move in, we had a spare bed for him to use, but Rae Marie and Matt took Yannick on a shopping spree to buy end tables, lamps, dishes, curtains, closet organizers, bed spreads, sheets, pillows, a TV and every household item that would make Yannick's apartment as cozy as possible. He finished the decorating with a beautiful painting that Yannick had drawn of his Mother. It honored his new home with the dignity of her memory and served as a reminder to Yannick from where and how far he had come.

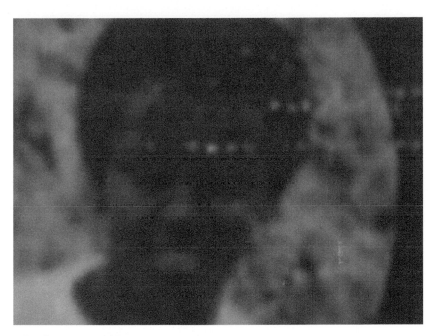

Claudine, Yannick's Mom, age 16

Peter with Beradi and Tracy and Yannick

Sonia, Aimee, Penti and Maurice Kabuguza

Dan Beirne and the Angels Army assemble the Kibeho Playground

Rwandan Children take the slides for a test ride

Tony Wieners, Gino Ambrosio, Brian Dolaghan and Kevin Kennedy with their newest friends

The Angels Army and the "Apostles" of Kibeho

The "Apostles" and their new wheels

Bill Lavin greets the Village of Kibeho at the Grand Opening

An arial view of Kibeho Playground

Dr. Patricia Fox and Dr. Jim Creighton with Yannick on the eve of his surgery

Chris and Shara McGowan, Charles Rwakabamba, Dickson Gomeko, Kathy and Bill Lavin

Yannick celebrates the U.S.A.

Matt Mitrow and Yannick in New York City

Rwanda's Playground testing crew

Yannick holds Matty while Marykate and Bill look on

CHAPTER TWENTY-SEVEN

I lift my Lamp beside the Golden Door

Yannick met with Alexandra Tseitlin, the Immigration Attorney. The United States was instituting via Presidential Executive Order the toughest immigration policy in generations. Anti-immigration rallies and rhetoric were at a fever pitch. Much of the political conversation centered on immigration reform. The chances of winning a case for asylum into the U.S. were about as difficult at any time in the country's history. We knew that preparing Yannick for his immigration application and interview was paramount.

Yannick and I would travel by train to Penn Station and walk a short two blocks to Alexandra Tseitlin's office. The first thing we needed to do was file for an extension of Yannick's medical visa.

Once the extension was granted, we knew we had about six months to prepare Yannick's application for asylum, as well as prepare him for his verbal in person interview.

The meetings we spent with Alexandra lasted three to four hours. Alexandra would interrogate Yannick about his childhood and the torture he had experienced throughout his youth. I thought I knew Yannick's story quite well but I had to admit, I really had not the first clue what Yannick saw and experienced at the hand of his attackers. It was so brutal, bloody and evil.

As Alexandra's questions became more personal and probing, Yannick would become extremely emotional and animated. Several times Yannick's retelling of the attack would bring him to tears, and he would tremble with sorrow as the agonizing experience was forced to replay in his mind.

Alexandra and I encouraged Yannick to stop and take a break in order to recollect his thoughts. Yannick refused and pressed on, as difficult as this was he wanted to verbalize it and get it over with quickly. As if it was a deep scar that he needed to rid himself. Yannick would confess to me that whenever he saw something or somebody that reminded him of his past, he would often have nightmares the following night. It was increasingly obvious, that in addition to his physical scars, Yannick was emotionally and psychologically scarred as well.

The affidavit was created, proof read, and edited many times until Yannick and Alexandra agreed it was not only accurate but would be an effective exhibit for the Immigration Office to review.

We held many subsequent meetings to discuss how Yannick would conduct himself and in which language he was most comfortable testifying and how much graphic information he should offer to the Immigration Officer.

Alexandra asked if I would agree to testify on Yannick's behalf as a character witness, as well as describe the support and network Yannick had in his corner.

Alexandra thought that the Immigration Office in New York would provide the more timely adjudication of his case, as well as perhaps be more sympathetic to his story. In order to be able to apply through the New York courts, Yannick would have to reside at a New York address. Thankfully our good friend and fellow "Angel Army" member, Gino Ambrosio, lives in Long Island. Gino was so gracious and more than happy to welcome Yannick into his home and provide the New York address necessary to accommodate Yannick's application. Gino was a great host allowing Yannick full access to his home and kept a close look out for correspondence from the Immigration Officer.

Gino took a great interest in Yannick's situation and offered advice as well as dinners, drinks and more importantly a roof over his head.

The night before Yannick's big interview he and I joined Gino for dinner. I stayed with Gino and Yannick overnight to accommodate the early morning appointment. Both Yannick and I were very nervous about our testimony, but much more was riding on Yannick's shoulders as his future literally hung in the balance. Yannick's interview was scheduled for early morning on the 18th of March, 2019.

We had a good laugh when I observed that this Irishman was celebrating St. Patrick's Day with an Italian and a Rwandan. Everyone is Irish on St. Patrick's Day! We had a couple of beers at Gino's favorite brewery, Spider Bites and then a great dinner at a nearby restaurant.

When we arrived back home to Gino's townhouse he suggested that he had the perfect movie to inspire Yannick for his interview. The film, *Rocky*, about the ultimate underdog is a great feel-good movie. Yannick seemed to really enjoy it. I told Yannick that Gino looked just like Sylvester Stallone when he was in his twenties. We told Yannick a few more stories to relax him and then we got an early night sleep. I'm sure Yannick tossed and turned most of the night as I know I did.

On March 18th, Yannick poured his heart out to an Immigration Officer whose first name was Fred. I took that as a great sign as my stepfather-in-law's name was Fred and he is now an Angel. Fred was born in England and immigrated to the United States and would have loved Yannick. I hoped and prayed that he was watching over Yannick that day. Several times Yannick broke down and cried as he answered the questions of why Rwanda held no place for him any longer. He was articulate and steady for most of the interview but passionate and emotional when the subject of his mother and grandparents was discussed.

I had the good fortune to be present in the room with Fred, the interviewer and was happy to hear the compelling case Yannick made. When it was my turn to testify I wanted Fred to know that I was aware of the politics of immigration that raged throughout our country. I asked Fred to consider Yannick's story and the uniqueness of his plight. Yet there were millions of people just like Yannick who longed for asylum into America, but probably none of them wore a scar on their face that identified them as an embarrassing historical reminder regarding their countrymen. Few would have to live in fear and be harassed every day in their native country, simply because they were a survivor the way that Yannick had.

I finished my testimony by suggesting to Fred that the United States of America was created precisely for people like Yannick. A country that gave people who were persecuted an opportunity to better themselves and be free. I also wanted Fred to understand my family, the Mitrow family, the "Angels Army," countless firefighters, police officers and I formed a resourceful network for Yannick to not only survive in America, I suggested he would thrive.

Alexandra let us know that she believed we did the best we could. Yannick left nothing on the table and we were all cautiously optimistic. The United States Citizenship and Immigration Services personnel informed us that Yannick would be notified of their decision on April 1st.

On April 1st, I was scheduled for a television interview with WUSA 9, the CBS affiliate that was promoting and financially sponsoring our next playground build in Gaithersburg, Maryland in honor of the Gemmell family. It was an appointment I was unable to re-schedule. I needed to promote the Where Angels Play Foundation project. As disappointing as it was for me, I would rely on Matt Mitrow and Gino Ambrosio to accompany Yannick when he received the most important decision of his life. Matt and Gino agreed and they all met at the Immigration Office that morning.

On April 1, 2018, while waiting in the CBS office to be interviewed, I got a call from Matt. He said and I quote, "Do you believe what this 'son of bitch' just did to me?" He continued, "He walks out of the office with a sad face and gives me the thumbs down!"

"Oh no that's terrible," I said.

"No, wait, there's more," Matt continued. "He lets me console him for a full minute, explaining how we will appeal, etc. I tell him not to get discouraged. Then he turns his thumbs down, to a thumbs up with a big grin."

Apparently Yannick knew about April 1st being April Fools Day and pulled a beauty on Matt.

Matt said, "I didn't know whether to smack him or hug him."

Then we laughed for quite some time. I was so happy for Yannick.

Yannick would be permitted to stay in America for at least the next five years and his life would never be the same!

I was just a little sad that I couldn't be with Yannick and Matt and Gino for what would prove to be a great celebration.

Mary Kate and I had to celebrate a few States away in honor of Yannick and the small miracle pulled off by Matt, Alexandra, Gino and a host of others.

Matt, Freddy, and Gino celebrate with Yannick after winning asylum

CHAPTER TWENTY-EIGHT

Land of Opportunity

So we had to start thinking about how Yannick would eventually support himself. I tried to get him a scholarship to Kean University in Union, New Jersey but that didn't quite pan out. Work would be important to keep Yannick busy and have him eventually achieve his independence. Yannick's employment would start slowly. One of our Angels Army members, Nancy Ur, offered Yannick a job doing odd jobs such as landscaping and yard work. It wasn't difficult but Nancy paid him well. Nancy Ur and her husband John have been great supporters of Where Angels Play Foundation. They are the Mom and Dad of an angel, John, as well as the grandparents of angel Owen Taraszkiewicz.

Nancy and John Ur, along with their daughter Megan and son-in-law Mark Taraszkiewicz, became a part of our family and the Angels Army team while building the Matawan-Aberdeen playground in honor of Owen.

From clothing to financial support, Nancy, John, Megan and Mark helped Yannick in any way they could.

One day I took Yannick to my favorite pizza place, Strawberry's Pub in Woodbridge, New Jersey. Our waitress' name was Angela, a lovely girl and always very friendly. I knew her from her job at Luciano's Restaurant in Rahway. Luciano's was a regular lunch and dinner meeting place for me when I was president of the NJFMBA. Our state office was just around the block. The following conversation always makes me laugh and is a great example of how so many word phrases and American gestures don't always translate exactly as they are meant. This will be another challenge for Yannick to overcome.

I asked Angela if she knew of any restaurants that might need a good worker like Yannick. I suggested maybe Luciano's because I knew Chef Joseph and spent quite a bit of time and money at that particular restaurant.

Angela replied, "I don't know about Yannick working there, they'll probably pay him peanuts."

I said, "Okay I'll check with Joseph nonetheless." I asked Angela to keep her eye open for a job for Yannick and she happily agreed.

When Angela left the table Yannick said, "Bill, why would that restaurant pay me in peanuts?"

"Oh no, Yannick they wouldn't really give you peanuts as payment. This is just an expression we use to mean a small sum of money," I said.

"Oh, that's a relief," Yannick said quite relieved. He continued, "You see, I have one tooth that has been hurting me and I can't chew peanuts."

He and I couldn't stop laughing. We had a great pizza and decided we would check out Luciano's—peanuts or not.

This is not the first time, however, that Yannick had complained about his tooth. I had wondered about dental care and if he had ever been to a dentist in his life. Of course, Yannick told me he had not. Another great supporter of the Where Angels Play Foundation was Karen Johnson. Karen had been married to one of our main playground builders, Mark Virag. Mark was the heart and soul of the cement team. Mark was now an Angel himself, after a twelve-year battle with cancer. He was and still is a legend with the Angels Army family. His story can be better learned in the "Where Angels Live, Work and Play" documentary book we published a few years back. Karen and her son Connor kept close contact with the foundation and would help out in any way they possibly could.

During a discussion with Yannick the subject of his tooth arose. He must have bitten on something that caused him obvious pain. Karen decided she would ask her dentist if he might be able to do a charitable deed and examine Yannick and perhaps fix his tooth. Dr. Paul Tedeschi of Edison Dental Arts was more than eager to help after Karen explained Yannick's story to him. Dr. Paul brought Yannick in for the first dental cleaning of his life and, he eventually extracted Yannick's bad tooth free of charge. This was another great act of kindness offered to our African visitor by a generous professional. Dr. Paul since has offered follow-up treatment for Yannick at no cost. There really are some great people in this country that you never hear about.

Yannick and I set up an appointment to see Chef Joseph at Luciano's and, after hearing his story, Joseph hired him on the spot. We thought it would work our perfect for Yannick as his apartment was only three blocks away from the restaurant. Soon Yannick was making $10 an hour and became the best dishwasher they ever had. He was always on time and worked as hard as he possibly could. Chef Joseph called me to say Yannick was fitting in fine and thanked me for recommending him as he was a great asset to the restaurant.

Yannick was now making real money in America and saving as much of it as he could. Language became an issue for Yannick as all the other kitchen staff spoke only Spanish. It was difficult for Yannick to communicate and get along with his co-workers at first. The language barrier was one thing, but he felt some resentment from them because he outworked all of them, rarely taking any breaks.

Yannick decided he already spoke five languages and thought he'd learn yet another in an effort to better communicate with his co-workers. He went on line and in a matter of six months was speaking conversational Spanish. He worked long hours—weekdays, weekends and holidays.

Soon he was working seven days a week. When he did get an occasional day off, we would meet at my house for dinner and he would fill me in.

I deposited Yannick's pay for him in a designated account until he was able to open a bank account for himself. Before long, he had saved

$5,000 US dollars. This was more money than he ever dreamed of having. On the rare days off, we would take Yannick to the Jersey shore where he saw the ocean for the first time. Matt also would have him over for dinner or take him into New York City for a fancy dinner or a night out.

But mostly Yannick would work and save and work and save. His new Spanish language skills would help him out with his co-workers but he never felt they truly accepted him. Yannick decided to stay at Luciano's until something else might come along.

Soon Yannick grew tired of the long hours of work with very little free time. We both felt that he was basically living at the restaurant and wasn't really experiencing the United States the way he should have been. Matt Mitrow had some contacts with the Architectural Window Company in Rutherford, New Jersey. It would be a better paying job and a little less physically taxing on him. The downside, however, was that he would travel by train two hours each day. He left Luciano's on good terms. They actually hated to see him go and offered him part time work if he ever wanted it.

Yannick started a new job at the Window plant in Rutherford. He was learning a lot about the manufacturing business, steel and window construction. His job was to make sure the correct steel was chosen for the right window project. He was a, sort of, quality assurance inspector. The job was not as physically demanding as the job at Luciano's had been but he had to stay on his toes. He enjoyed the work, as it was much different than the hot steam of the dishwasher and hustle and bustle of the kitchen at Luciano's. Here he found a very diverse work force... black, Latino, white and Asian. There were almost 600 employees, so Yannick made friends more easily now and felt more a part of a team.

Taking the train every day was expensive, however, and he soon realized that with travel he wasn't really making much more money than he was at Luciano's. Yannick researched how to get a driver's license and studied the online test.

Independently, Yannick applied for and earned his New Jersey driver's permit and license.

He would now have the freedom to purchase his own car with the money he saved. As we started looking around for a nice small fuel-efficient car for Yannick that would be safe and economical, Yannick had some ideas of his own.

Apparently a co-worker at the window factory had a used pick-up truck that he offered to sell Yannick. Yannick made the deal for a 2004 rusty old gas eating pick-up truck and was pretty proud of the purchase he had made, that was until he realized that he was constantly pumping gas into it. If he thought the train was expensive, he soon realized using the New Jersey Turnpike daily was even worse. This would take an even bigger chunk out of his entry-level salary at the window factory.

Riding on the New Jersey Turnpike was no walk in the park either. It wasn't long before Yannick was back to taking two trains to work and the truck sat mostly unused in his apartment complex parking lot. This proved to be a valuable but rather expensive lesson for Yannick. Yannick had not yet learned the expression "I told you so" and neither Matt nor I had the heart to teach him... at least not yet!

The people at Architectural Window Company were treating Yannick much better than his co-workers at Luciano's ever did, and he was making some friends. He began to realize, however, that for all his hard work he still was barely making ends meet. So after a long talk with Matt it was agreed that Yannick would leave his job and attend a three-month school in Manhattan to study graphic design. Once again the ever-generous Matt would support Yannick's education. Matt had a long-term plan for Yannick. He would attend Shillington, a first rate Graphic Design School, and upon graduation he would come to work at Matt's company, Blue Ladder Inc. Yannick was a quick learner, loved the computer and was a talented artist. We had little doubt he would excel at the school and upon completion he would have a certificate in Graphic Design that would make Yannick a marketable commodity in that industry.

He could further his education with Matt's business and get on the job training. Yannick's life would change for the better once again. He soon became quite knowledgeable about train and subway schedules in and around the biggest and busiest city in the world—New York.

Yannick started to feel challenged and alive with possibilities. He was eager to show us his work and ever growing portfolio and skills. Yannick even offered to reconstruct the Where Angels Play Foundation's website. Yannick was now studying with the best and brightest in this field. His classmates would inspire him and challenge him intellectually and socially. Now instead of slowing down his work and dumbing down his conversation, Yannick shared his schoolwork projects and his new skills with classmates. He was still unique and different in the melting pot that is New York City but, then again, so was everyone else in his class and all around this bustling metropolis.

In March 2020, all was going well and nothing he could imagine would stand in his way and then Covid-19 hit. Not watching news as a rule, or reading newspapers much, Yannick was so focused on his studies and his projects he didn't see the global pandemic coming until it was too late. Before noticing and understanding why so many people on the train and walking on the streets of Manhattan were wearing facemasks, Yannick began to feel sick.

I made one of my routine calls to Yannick late in the evening and he sounded terrible. He told me he was very hot, couldn't stop sweating and was coughing non-stop. I knew right away he had been infected with the Coronavirus.

Thankfully, the Where Angels Play network included Patrick Wildridge and his wife Nicole Keegan. Nicole a doctor at Monmouth Medical Center had tested positive for Covid-19 herself, and was our "go-to" for advice and counsel regarding the Coronavirus. Nicole was terrific with Yannick advising him on what to do and how to best handle his symptoms. Yannick eventually went to the hospital for a check up but at the time the Rahway Hospital was full to capacity. They told Yannick, if he could walk in to the Emergency Room then he was not sick enough for them to treat. That is how dire the circumstances were in New Jersey at that time.

Nicole was able to monitor and advise Yannick over the phone and nurtured him back to health from a distance.

I was able to drop off some food, supplies, masks and Tylenol for Yannick and hoped for the best. It was heartbreaking to see him suffering. He was so sick and weak. I felt helpless to not be able to do anything for him. Nicole kept close tabs on Yannick and so many others. It seemed the entire State of New Jersey was in the same boat. No one wanted to leave their homes except to shop and get drugs from the pharmacy.

Slowly, Yannick started to come around and his fever broke and eventually his lungs cleared up. He was young and strong and was able to defeat the Coronavirus. After all, Yannick had been through so much worse. It would have been a great injustice for him to come so far to succumb to this insidious disease.

As the state and country argued over how to deal with the pandemic, Yannick finished his Graphic Design School from home. Shillington School had gone to remote learning and Yannick was able to graduate with a certificate as a graphic designer. He shared his portfolio with my family and me. It was so impressive. It was obvious he had a bright future in front of him.

Dr. Paul Tedeschi, Karen and Connor Johnson with Brigida at Yannick's first visit

CHAPTER TWENTY-NINE

Racial Unrest, Social Justice, Police Under Siege

If the Coronavirus Pandemic and an economic lockdown weren't enough for us all to deal with, the murder of George Floyd sparked protests and racial unrest I hadn't seen since the 1960s. This brutal video of a police officer kneeling on a black man's neck and snuffing his life out disgusted everyone across America. This action placed police and law enforcement under a microscope like never before. Black Lives Matter protests turned violent and destructive. Looting and rioting drowned out peaceful protests and inner cities across the United States erupted into fiery war zones.

Yannick watched the news in disgust and confusion. He struggled to understand what was happening to the country he had long dreamt about. When Yannick first came to live with us in Woodbridge, my son-in-law Matt Herbert stopped over our house to meet Yannick to welcome him. Matt was an undercover detective with the Woodbridge Police Department and came into the house with his service gun on his hip. As soon as Yannick noticed the gun, he became frightened until Matt assured him that it was part of his job and posed no danger to Yannick. Nevertheless, Yannick was uneasy about the gun and was clearly uncomfortable.

Yannick's history in Rwanda left him psychologically scarred, and he maintained a healthy respect and fear of guns. Yannick grew to know Matt and many other police officers in our network of family and friends and better understood their place in American society. He did not fully understand the role of police in America as compared to the role of police in Rwanda.

The murder of George Floyd by a uniformed police officer in Minneapolis ignited racial unrest across the country and did nothing to ease Yannick's mind or further his understanding. Like many of us, Yannick was confused and frightened by the rioting and destruction in many parts of the country. Stories of police involved shootings and the madness depicted in cities defied reason. Yannick emailed me a video of black men and women rioters and looters breaking store front windows and stealing sneakers and sportswear from department stores in downtown New York City. His caption read, "Why are these people stealing and rioting?" He further asked, "What does this have to do with the murder of George Floyd?" Obviously I had no credible explanation. The truth was that I had lived in the United States for 62 years and I was struggling to make any sense of the actions of so many people as the civil unrest raged across our country.

If I had trouble making sense of what was happening to our nation how much more confusing would it be for Yannick? He told me that in Rwanda things would be handled with great force. I could only suggest to Yannick that what makes our country great also makes it very complex and complicated.

Of course we didn't want to have lawlessness, looting and rioting in the streets and yet we didn't want the execution of those who would violate the law. This conversation really did underscore the difficult position facing police and society as a whole. Eliminating and prosecuting the unjust police activity of a few brutal officers while supporting and respecting the vast majority of great civil servants who are tasked with the toughest job in America is the challenge of our lifetime.

Yannick would continue to read and watch the political division that was threatening to tear America apart.

When the pandemic appeared to slow down in New Jersey after the deaths of over 14,000 people state wide and almost 215,000 nationwide,

Yannick felt the need to get back to work. The economy was at its worst since the Great Depression of 1929, finding graphic designer work was proving quite impossible. Yannick felt the need to work and saw an ad online for Amazon distribution center in nearby Avenel, New Jersey.

Without me even knowing about it, Yannick applied and was hired as a scanner. He was excited to be called an Amazonian and to be part of the largest company in the world. Yannick put his best foot forward and dove headfirst into the hectic world of scanning packages at a workstation alongside of hundreds of other Amazon employees. Yannick was once again making $15 an hour but he was excited to be part of a big workforce and would soon earn health benefits and employee benefits he had never before been afforded.

After three months when he received his health benefit card he couldn't wait to show me. He was excited to have his very own health benefits and wanted to use them for physicals, prescriptions and dental work just like any hardworking American. He was so proud of what he was accomplishing. He soon would face the wrath of the American worker, however, and be confronted with another American social reality.

Yannick was working as fast and as hard as he could as he always did. If the average career Amazon worker was scanning 200 to 300 packages a day, Yannick was scanning 1,000 packages. So Yannick was so proud and happy to tell me that he had earned a $50 Amazon Gift Card as a bonus.

We were happy for Yannick and proud he was excelling in his new job even if it was only this entry level scanning position. After a week or so, I asked Yannick how the job was going and he said it was ok but some of the other employees were suddenly not treating him so nice. Apparently when Yannick received his bonus reward for working so hard, it was reported and announced on his computer screen as well as the workstation screens of all the other employees. Out of jealousy or feeling threatened that Yannick was making the other workers look bad, they began to shun him in the break room and at lunch.

Some of the comments he received included, "Congratulations, you're making Bezos a rich man," or, "What's wrong with you, are you an Amazon slave?"

They remarked, "Take it easy, boy, you don't want to get hurt."

Yannick was hurt and confused of course when he came to dinner one night.

He asked me, "Bill, what does dumb ass n_____ mean?"

I said, "Yannick where did you hear that?"

He sadly replied, "That's what some of my co-workers call me, but I've never heard that phrase before."

I was crushed and hurt for Yannick and angry, actually. I tried my best to explain that is a terrible word and a very demeaning phrase. I also explained why another black man using that word is sometimes accepted in our culture but that I, or another white man, could never say that without it being completely offensive. Of course it took a while for him to understand, and finally I'm not sure he fully understood.

He also sometimes heard phrases like, "What's up my n_____?"

I tried to explain that phrase is actually considered by some to be an acceptable greeting from one black man to another but certainly "a dumb ass n_____" was offensive when said by any race, color or creed.

Needless to say it would take a long time for Yannick to understand this complex use of the English language and its use by different ethnicities and cultures.

The nuances of language and American slang and part of our English lexicon are difficult to comprehend on their own. Then to further understand the complex nature of race relations and social norms and what is considered acceptable and politically correct is difficult enough for an American—black or white. Consider the additional burden for a twenty-nine year old Rwandan trying to navigate the complexities of ever-changing American culture.

So Yannick decided to slow down his daily work output to more closely align with what his fellow employees thought was appropriate and sure enough they began to treat him better. Perhaps a sad commentary on the American work ethic, but Yannick decided it was less stressful to comply with his peers and it was easier to just get along. There really was no human interaction with management or supervisors, so what was the point other than losing the bonus incentives. Yannick got his first lesson in American worker peer pressure.

I did assure him that he was grossly overqualified for his position.

His intelligence and ability to now speak six languages was proof positive he was the furthest thing from being considered a dumb ass of any kind and it would be advisable to forget he ever heard the "N" word and never to use it again.

I knew that when Yannick got into the corporate world as a graphic design artist, he would be able to work as hard and as long and as dedicated as he liked and it would benefit him greatly unlike his experience at his current job scanning packages for Amazon.

Yannick battles COVID-19

CHAPTER THIRTY

Climbing out of the Cellar

After two years, three jobs, and a successful graphic design school graduation, Yannick kept his nose to the grindstone. He worked long and hard at Amazon and had amassed as much money as he could. He was able to walk to and from work, about a thirty-minute hike. Yannick was saving on trains, gasoline, and Uber rides. He made some friends, and life was just ok. I asked Yannick if he had met any girls at work, that he might be interested in dating.

He said plainly, "I have but I don't really know what they look like, or if they have any teeth because everyone wears a mask all the time."

We both cracked up laughing. I guess the coronavirus pandemic is not the best circumstance for anyone trying to join the dating scene.

With the Coronavirus plaguing the country and the worst economy in decades, the prospects for Yannick's future employment were not looking promising at all.

Yannick had to be wondering what could possibly happen next to turn his dream country into a nightmare. In Yannick's own personal sphere of existence, things were rapidly taking a turn for the worse. The studio apartment where he has been living was the basement of a three-story garden apartment complex. This building was getting more and more seedy and overcrowded with rowdy and unruly neighbors.

Loud music, late night parties, trash littering the hallways, suspected drug use and distribution appeared to be more and more commonplace.

When I dropped off some groceries for Yannick one evening, I noticed at least eight or nine pairs of shoes lining the wall outside the door across the hallway from his apartment. When I asked him about it he just shook his head.

He whispered, "You have no idea what life is like here at night."

Yannick told me, he didn't want to complain, because Matt Mitrow was so generous helping him with his rent.

He said, "At least I'm not in Rwanda."

I felt bad for Yannick and thought we have to start looking out for a more civil and safe place for him to live.

One night, about a week later, I received a text at 2:30 a.m. from Yannick that read, "Hey Buddy, let me move out next month, please. Can't even sleep... thank you." I told him to hang in there, and I would call him the next day.

Yannick explained that teenage kids, ages 17 and 18, were banging on his door and walls, threatening him saying, "We're gonna kill that n_____." This family is black as well and this behavior made no sense other than to harass him and make his life miserable. I became truly concerned for his safety at that point. Yannick was struggling at work, because he wasn't getting much sleep due to this untenable situation at his home.

After speaking with Yannick and visiting his apartment, I grew concerned for his safety. There was a distinct drop off in cleanliness around his building. The litter outside the building and inside the hallways was out of control. Used masks were strewn everywhere, liquor bottles and discarded beer cans were everywhere. Yannick explained that the drug use in and around his apartment was becoming commonplace.

I started making some calls to have our network of friends, keep their eyes open for a safer, more permanent place where Yannick could feel more at ease and at least get a good night's sleep. I spoke with Matt Mitrow, and he agreed, it was time to make a move.

John Boyle of Boyle Real Estate has been a long time friend and ally of the the Where Angels Play Foundation, as well as the New Jersey

State FMBA. He is a brilliant guy, with brilliant children, all patriots, and just salt of the earth. John was a regular member in the many Irish Associations in Union County and around the State of New Jersey. So it was natural that I shared Yannick's story with him and I knew he would be moved by it. John had many resources and connections in the real estate world and he said he would get on the phone and see what options were available for Yannick.

Within hours I heard back from one of the best real estate attorneys in New Jersey, a man named Andrew Ullrich. I had met Andrew through John earlier in the year and he was quite familiar with the Where Angels Play Foundation and the work we have been blessed to do. Andrew listened to Yannick's story and enthusiastically took on the challenge to find him the best possible living space at the best possible price.

In a matter of days, Andrew had found a beautiful place in Edison, New Jersey. It was a great area surrounded by shops and restaurants. This area was a safer neighborhood and the apartments were clean and well maintained. Yannick was excited to move. He first saw the place with Matt Mitrow... they both agreed this was the perfect place for Yannick. So the news was good for Yannick and getting better every day.

October 2020 would be a most important month for Yannick. A new apartment in a new town would soon be available. Then Yannick received word that a new job was now available in his field of graphic design at Blue Ladder Marketing. He would now be getting a chance to work in a field he loved. A job where no one would ever tell him to slow down or be less than he wanted to be. He now had a job that he would excel in and be appreciated for his professionalism and hard work. He called it his dream job.

To complete Yannick's October trifecta he would also be receiving a company car as well. A new home, job and car... all in the same month, life was finally shining bright.

"This is America!" Yannick shouted joyfully.

The future had never been brighter!

John Boyle, Yannick, Bill and Chris Dickerson celebrate a new living space for Yannick

"The Starfish"

CHAPTER THIRTY-ONE

Sweet Land of Liberty of Thee I Sing

Today is October 14, 2020, and I write this final chapter on the beautiful beach of Ocean Grove, New Jersey. Today the town of Randolph, Massachusetts received the delivery of a playground that will one day soon be constructed to honor Dennis "DJ" Simmonds. DJ Simmonds is a hero Boston Police Officer, who gave his life, as a result of injuries sustained during the capture of the Boston Marathon bombers.

I'm sad because that playground build was supposed to start today. The Where Angels Play Foundation was forced to postpone this project until the spring because of the Covid-19 pandemic.

To say 2020 has been a difficult year for America would be a gross understatement.

Today we are exactly three weeks from the most contentious presidential election in generations.

The Covid-19 pandemic has already taken over 215,000 American lives and a second wave is about to accelerate the virus all across the country. The economy is a mess, and the joblessness rate is growing daily. Civil unrest is occurring everywhere. Protests against police are almost daily. Rallies to support police, and law and order, attempt to counter the "defunding movement." All of which continue to devolve into rioting, looting and violence. Social justice is juxtaposed against law and order. Wildfires are burning out of control in the West, hurricanes are relentlessly pounding the Gulf States, and tornadoes and flooding are devastating the Midwest.

Neighboring New York City is deteriorating. Crime and homelessness is evident everywhere. Black Lives Matter dominates the headlines, while White Supremacists' attempt to kidnap the sitting Governor of Michigan. Not to mention, a controversial confirmation hearing for a new Supreme Court Justice.

Did I forget to mention Murder Hornets?

Facebook, Twitter, Instagram, Tik Tok and Snap Chat, provide a forum for unchecked, unsubstantiated opinions and invective. Hate speech seems everywhere.

Maybe it is not the most ideal time, to assimilate a young Rwandan Genocide survivor, to our, "Sea to Shining Sea." Or is it?

Yannick arrived here in the United States to have the best medical treatment in the world. A brilliant plastic surgeon unselfishly lent her considerable skills and resources to give Yannick a whole new life and identity.

Doctors, nurses, hospital administrators, firefighters, teachers and police officers offered charity, love, compassion and understanding.

Businesses and charitable foundations, offered money, food and housing. My friends and family, as well as complete strangers, opened up their homes, wallets and hearts to Yannick.

I realized the America, being reported on the television channels, is what I was ashamed of—not the America I actually live in every day.

While the news reports unrest and division, my America was working with grieving families to bring them healing, joy and celebration to their Angels.

The America Yannick was experiencing was of caring, kind attorneys who shepherded his case through a compassionate Immigration Officer's hands.

My America was celebrating Yannick's first birthday, his first barbecue, his first Thanksgiving dinner and first Christmas morning.

My America was providing Yannick's first oral surgery and first teeth cleaning by a compassionate, generous and talented dentist all at no cost.

My America was caring, kind and inclusive. My police, fire and government employee unions were listening to Yannick, honoring, including and nurturing him.

This is the America Yannick is experiencing, despite what he, and we, are trying to understand from our nightly news program.

This is the reminder I needed, about my America in 2020, and it gives me hope for our future and the future of my grandchildren born and unborn.

This is what my America did for Yannick and why I am so proud, *still* to be an American.

What Yannick did for me and everyone else he met in America, is what gives me even more hope, for Yannick and the world.

We should all take the time to see our America through Yannick Kabuguza's eyes.

Yannick taught forgiveness to our labor unions.

Yannick taught appreciation to our high school students.

Yannick taught the joy and preciousness of a birthday celebration with family no matter what gift you may receive.

Yannick taught me the value of a good job, safe home, and a pimped out man cave.

Yannick taught us the joy of holding a child of another race.

Yannick taught us what real adversity looks like, what a real problem is, and the difference between a problem and a mere inconvenience.

Yannick brings out the best in people and he did that for my family and me.

Yannick's story and journey showcased the best about my America, and your America, if you'll only take the time to know him, and the uplifting and healing message of forgiveness he embodies.

I wish him success, joy, family and happiness, all the things he's already given to me and to everyone who comes in contact with him.

Yannick spends a great deal of time counting his blessings, and appreciating his new-found good fortune.

Yannick thanks me and Matt and Kathy and Rae Marie and many others every day, I suppose he has an inclination and right to do so.

However, each and every character in this book who has been thanked by Yannick will agree with me that we are the grateful ones and Yannick is the one we should be thanking.

What we as Americans have given Yannick makes me proud to call the United States my home, my country, and my people.

What Yannick has given to America makes me glad I've had the privilege of meeting him and knowing his story.

I believe we were placed in Yannick's path at the best time for him to fulfill his dream of coming to America. It is without any doubt that Yannick was placed in our path at the precise moment we needed him to remind us of the greatness of America. I believe only God could have made it all happen.

Where are they now?

The Where Angels Play Foundation continues to build playgrounds for Angels with the support of so many great businesses and grass roots volunteers. Every member of the "Angels Army" described in this book continues to work alongside the countless members of the foundation who are not mentioned in this writing but are equally remarkable.

Scarlett Lewis and the Jesse Lewis Choose Love Foundation continue to change the world through education and social and emotional learning!

Rebecca and Steve Kowalski continue to impact thousands of children through the Race for Chase Foundation! Dave Fowler and Bike for Kids provide the joy of bicycles to underprivileged children everywhere.

Nancy and John Ur and Megan and Mark Taraskiewicz continue to support children's charities across America in Owen's name!

Alexandra Tseitlin continues to win freedom for worthy immigrants and change the fortunes of countless people.

The New Jersey Firefighters Mutual Benevolent Association, now led by president Ed Donnelly, continues to be the model union representing Firefighters and their families throughout New Jersey.

Gino Ambrosio continues to work as a nurse at Memorial Sloan Kettering in Commack, New York, lives on Long Island, promotes Where Angels Play Foundation, keeps in touch with Yannick and watches the movie *Rocky* at least every couple of months.

The National Association of Government Employees, N.A.G.E., led by David Holway, continues to grow nationally as an advocate for working families everywhere.

Dr. Paul Tedeschi continues to serve the people in and around Edison with the finest dental healthcare imaginable.

Dr. Patricia Fox continues to provide brilliant health care and compassion to her patients in Schenectady, New York.

Dr. Jim Creighton and Gene MacDonald, along with Sean, Palesa and Caroline are currently living in New Zealand. Jim is applying for a PhD in Science Communication and Gene is applying for a PhD in Climate Change. They continue to change the world for the better in so many ways.

Tim Huber and Heather Waters continue to teach at their respective high schools and shape the young minds in their charge, focusing on appreciation and forgiveness!

Maurice continues to work in the film industry in Rwanda, France and the United States.

Aimee lives in the town of Rebero, Rwanda, with her younger brother Penti and her two children Sacha and Amariza.

Sister Bridget and Sister Emilene continue to operate the Mother of the Word School in Kibeho providing education and possibilities for their students.

The "apostles" are considered to be legends by some in Kibeho, as they navigate the dirt roads and countryside in and around Kibeho on their bicycles!

Goretti continues to work in Law Enforcement and enjoys the love and appreciation from Yannick for helping him when he needed it most.

Peter has found God through the bible, has sought and received Yannick's forgiveness and lives a contented life in Kigali.

Karigo lives in Burundi and is happily married with children of her own.

Jean Paul is raising two children and trying to make ends meet in a difficult economy in Kigali, Rwanda. He keeps in touch with Where Angels Play Foundation and its members regularly.

Matt and Rae Marie Mitrow and their family are working success-ful careers while they continue to share their lives with Yannick and many other young souls who need a helping hand.

Kayibanda continues to serve his life sentence for the atrocities he committed during the genocide. He is comforted, however, by the knowledge he has been forgiven by Yannick.

The Lavin family and the Where Angels Play Foundation contin-ue to sing the long version of "Happy Birthday"(five songs in all), for their family and extended family whenever possible. On the 28th of September it is sung especially loud to make up for lost time!

And Yannick Kabuguza... lives in Edison, New Jersey, studying in the field of Graphic Design, working hard and saving for his future and the future of Starfish from Rwanda, who are waiting for him to bend down, pick them up and hurl them in to salvation.

Epilogue

As the title of this book and accompanying story suggest, there are so many people in Africa and around the world in need of saving. The message I hope this book delivered is, while one person cannot save all—all can save one!

The group that visited Rwanda to build a playground sought to make a difference for the community as a whole. A common theme emerged among our volunteers that we wished we could save every child we encountered and provide for them a better life.

The story of Yannick symbolizes what is possible. When I take in to account all the things that occurred on this journey, and the timing of each and every one of them, it is impossible for me to deny the influence of angels and the power of the faith in God.

The strength and resilience of Yannick and the generosity and sacrifice of so many others in this story shouted to me, above all the noise, that people can be so good to one another. Maybe we need to be reminded of how blessed we are as compared to so many others in this world. The lessons we can learn from the difficulties in our lives are boundless.

A recent television drama suggested to me that, "the tragedies of our lives are the fence posts on which the rest of our lives are hung." They serve as foundations to string a life of resilience, forgiveness, appreciation and love for one another.

Yannick's future and the future of us all will be determined by how we respond to the challenges before us and the empathy and understanding we provide to one another.

Acknowledgements

To Eileen Barbieri, Joyce Adase and Judy Lavin for previewing early text and making valuable recommendations.

To Nancy Ur, whose skill, advice and friendship made this book considerably more readable and organized.

To Charles W. Lavin, "Butch;" Thank you for agreeing to be the Chief Managing Editor and your time and attention to detail.

To MaryKate Herbert, Executive Director of Where Angels Play Foundation, thank you for keeping the foundation on the cutting edge of healing, hope and recovery.

To Kathy Lavin, thank you for the countless hours of writing and translating and advising every note and piece of information necessary to make this story possible.

To Deidra Stierle, thank you for setting this book in position for success.

To Yannick Kabuguza, the Starfish from Africa, for sharing your remarkable story of courage, faith and forgiveness with the world.

To the "Angels Army," for being the foundation of the Where Angels Play Foundation.